Thirty Days with America's High School Coaches

Martin A. Davis Jr.

To learn more about this book and its author, please visit:

www.MartinDavisAuthor.com

www.ThirtyDaysWith.com

Cover design and illustration by Rick Nease
www.RickNeaseArt.com

Published by
Front Edge Publishing
42807 Ford Road, Suite 234
Canton, MI, 48187

Front Edge Publishing books are available for discount bulk purchases
for events, corporate use and small groups. Special editions, including
books with corporate logos, personalized covers and customized interi-
ors are available for purchase. For more information, contact Front Edge
Publishing at info@FrontEdgePublishing.com

To Thelma, the greatest coach a man could hope for;
To Andrew, who taught me to see the beauty of baseball anew;
To Katie, who taught me the limits of sport;
And to Austin, who lived sports as few of us are able,
and brought me along for the ride.

Contents

Praise for *Thirty Days with America's High School Coaches*

Martin Davis has written a book that highlights the impact that high school coaches have on the lives of their athletes. The key to success both on and off the field are the relationships that each of these coaches have with their players, which extends well beyond a student's high school career. This is a textbook on the value that high school coaches bring to a school community. This is a great read as well as a valuable resource for all coaches, athletes, parents and administrators.

Steve Young, CMAA, Director of Athletics, City School District of New Rochelle, New Rochelle, NY.

Coaches and athletic administrators nationwide will find that this book can generate helpful conversations about how to hone our crafts and identify best practices in our profession. Although the stories behind the successes of the coaches profiled in this book are unique, they are nevertheless equally inspirational. Reading about these coaches, it becomes very clear how they have made a difference in the lives of the young people in their charge. Davis clearly illustrates the importance of relationships, program culture, community involvement and investment, and program philosophy in guiding these coaches. At its core, Davis's work reveals that the true essence of coaching is teaching and that the most effective coaches are those who forge connections with their student-athletes. The impact of each of the coaches described in this book extends far beyond the playing fields and courts; they are purveyors of lessons and skills that have transformed lives.

Gary Stevens, Athletic Administrator, Thornton Academy, Saco, Maine, and Assistant Director of the Maine Interscholastic Athletic Administrators Association.

I once knew a coach who failed—at swearing. When he got angry, he'd often blurt out this: "By damn …" By damn? Instead of paying attention to what we players had just done wrong, we had to work hard to hold in our laughter. What this man needed was this new book by Marty Davis. Not that it would have taught him to swear. But it would have reminded him why he was a coach in the first place: Not to win games but to give healthy, generative direction to young lives. Any coach who can learn that from this book will—no matter his or her final won-loss record—be a great coach, by damn.

Bill Tammeus is the author of *Love, Loss and Endurance: A 9/11 Story of Resilience and Hope in an Age of Anxiety* and is a past president of the National Society of Newspaper Columnists.

Martin Davis has a deep understanding of the lasting impression, both positive and negative, that a high school coach can have on teenage student-athletes. There is something to be learned from each coach Martin includes in this collection of 30 true stories. These are gems that show us how coaches can come to love and inspire their student-athletes. If you want to be inspired, this is a must read!

Michael J. Groves is the President of EMC Planning Group, a land use and environmental planning firm and is Head Baseball Coach for Monterey High School.

High school sports are an idea as unique as America itself. The dedicated men and women who coach our children live at the intersection of family, school, and community life. They are all over-worked, and in most cases underpaid. Their reward comes in the form of seeing young people reach their potential, in and out of sport. In his book, Martin Davis provides a never-before-seen insider's perspective of the power coaches can have on youth, schools, and communities in America. Through his reporting,

Davis shares insight into what makes America's high school coaches successful across sports, school types, and communities. More than that, he highlights real-world examples of what allows coaches to excel across their many roles. This book is a must read not only for coaches, but for coach educators, school administrators, and community leaders as well.
Travis Dorsch, Ph.D., Founding Director Utah State University Families in Sport Lab.

The vocation of being a coach is central to the life of so many young people. Coaches impact their players on so many levels, which in turn creates enormous responsibility. Martin Davis' book is an important read for anyone who possesses the job title: Coach. This book offers quick wisdom that will last a lifetime and impact many young athletes for years to come. You don't have to be an elite college or professional coach to make a difference and the stories of these coaches in this book remind us all of the vital role we play when add the word Coach to our name.
Jen Brooks, CMAA, Athletic Director, Ursuline Academy, Saint Louis, Missouri.

Thirty Days with America's High School Coaches is a must read for all who hold dearly our formative years in sports. I personally appreciate and recognize the important role my coaches had as influencers and mentors. They left indelible imprints on my life, teaching me valuable lessons about teamwork, vision, decision-making, endurance, values of winning and the lessons of losing, honor, and sportsmanship.
Howard Brown, author of *Shining Brightly*.

Foreword

Long before reporters had to shoehorn their best insights into choppy blog-posts and pithy tweets, they had access to a journalistic genre known as the "appreciation." It was neither a news story nor an editorial. Appreciations artfully recognized contributions of unsung locals and quietly impactful organizations. Readers loved them, and why not? What had always been precious to their communities finally was being honored publicly. Tributes to shared values, commitments and lessons are indeed appreciated.

In Thirty Days with America's High School Coaches, Martin Davis dusts off the appreciation genre for a subject near to his heart. In 30 mini-profiles, he celebrates what high school coaches do when plying their crafts. These curated moments, gleaned from interviews exploring dozens of coach-player relationships, take readers inside dynamics that change lives for the better.

Davis comes by his study honestly. Adding football coach to his resume in middle age meant he needed to learn fast. He tapped his research skills as a scholar and journalist. His economical writing style and eye for telling details serve his project well.

But Davis brings his greatest value to the project when making editorial decisions about what belongs in these profiles. He mines hours of interviews for golden moments that capture what made an enduring difference for a young person. Readers begin to absorb what it meant, for instance, when a coach contacted every player's family after a tornado ripped through town. And what it meant for a football coach to befriend a non-athlete who'd lacked confidence. And what it meant for a basketball coach to scrap her long list of rules and trust her players to do the right thing.

From these interviews and vignettes come narratives that will keep coaches going—even on days when players are ready to quit. They will quench the thirsts of professionals eager to drink from a well of peers' stories. They pack practical insights for how to build the trust and confidence that teenagers deeply crave and need.

Although the book is explicitly about coaching high school sports, it delivers many a transferable insight for parents, teachers, pastors and others who'd like to engage the teens in their lives more effectively.

Who couldn't use more of that? How good coaches go about showing that they genuinely care can be instructive for just about anyone.

In Davis' hands, the art of appreciating coaches is never trite or predictable. It's constantly shedding new light on what matters most in his eyes. It's a rare coach who can put the craft into words. It's an even rarer one who can be a conduit for sharing his fellow coaches' stories as well. Davis' book shows he's up to the challenge on all fronts and makes a solid contribution to coaching literature.

For more than two decades, journalist G. Jeffrey MacDonald has focused his reporting on religion, ethics and social responsibility. His stories have appeared in *TIME*, *The Washington Post*, *USA Today*, *The Boston Globe* and *The Christian Science Monitor*. You can learn more about his work at gjeffreymacdonald.com.

Preface

I'm a hardcore professor of sport coaching. I write a lot of long research papers with big words, which most people don't read. For over a dozen years now, I've taught college students what, why and how to coach.

Now, I'll be using the stories in this book to show what sport coaching is all about. We will discuss the culture, time period, and psychology of the coaches and the storytellers in this book. We will compare it to research on sport coaches and coach-athlete relationships, coach development, coaching philosophy, and the social foundations of sport in society.

Through short stories that ring true, this book brings to life so much of what I try to convey and discuss with students and coaches.

As a professor, I critique everything and I could critique varies odds and ends of the book, but I've learned to discern wisdom when I see it. Years ago, I once said that the best coaches are the best actors and storytellers. Davis's storytellers provide moving testimony on what coaching should be about.

The stories are pearls of wisdom for new and experienced coaches, as well as leaders and just people in general. I wasn't but two pages in when I started shaking my head affirmatively. There is truthfulness and authenticity in the writing. The pages are full of honest coach-speak about the realities of coaching, including kids with cancer and mental health problems, failure, success, humility, legacy, poverty, inequality, growth and learning—and on and on with stories of everyday high school coaching. *Thirty Days with America's High School Coaches* is packed with practical, powerful stories that you'll be glad you read.

Much of this book is about leadership and the ideals we want to uphold. I've already taken away a new lesson that I'll use with my own son as I coach his 7th grade tackle football team. At my suggestion, my son is trying to figure out how to be a leader. He is going to have to learn to fail and be vulnerable enough to fail. Coach Fracassa, who is highlighted in several instances throughout the book, quotes from Teddy Roosevelt's The Man in the Arena speech, "Guys in life who are afraid to fail never do anything."

Tell that to a 12-year-old!

Well, OK, I will.

That's what coaches do—we find ways to coach up lessons on and off the field, improving ourselves as we improve others and the communities we live. That's what this book and coaching is all about.

Dr. Brian Gearity, PhD, CSCS, FNSCA, ATC, is a coach and a tenured professor at the University of Denver, where he also is the director of Online Graduate Sport Degrees and Undergraduate Kinesiology and Sport Studies.

Introduction

When it comes to shaping America's next generation, high school coaches may well be the most important people in our society.

If that statement seems over-the-top, consider this: Research shows that students who engage in athletics not only tend to do better in school, but that the lessons they learn from sports and their high school coaches stay with them long after they've left high school. Further, according to research gathered by the National Federation of State High School Associations, high school student-athletes tend to have fewer mental health issues later in life, do better in their work careers, vote more regularly, and volunteer more than students who don't play interscholastic sports. More interesting, these findings generally apply to students of all socioeconomic statuses, races, and family backgrounds.

Yet one doesn't need to review 20 years of academic research to appreciate the profound impact that high school coaches can have. Just spend some time talking with those who played high school sports. The person who doesn't remember their high school coach and the lessons that person taught them is an anomaly.

What are high school coaches doing that makes them so successful in working with 14- to 18-year-olds?

I've watched high school coaches through a number of lenses in my life: as a parent, as a journalist, and most important, perhaps, as a coach myself. My interactions with these individuals and my own experiences as a coach have furthered my belief that this question deserves more attention than it traditionally receives.

Over the past year, I've sought out and spoken with high school coaches across the country, asking them how they do what they do. Some of these coaches are well-known in their communities and celebrated for their success in winning championships; others are just starting out or have labored under the radar for years.

These coaches specialize in more than a dozen varsity sports. They're in elite private schools, sprawling suburban high schools and inner-city campuses. Some enjoyed an elite education, while others came up through the school of hard knocks. Some were standout athletes themselves in high school and college, although most were not. They are Asian, Latino, Black and white; male and female; well-compensated, working on small stipends, and serving as volunteers.

Yet for all their differences, it's the things they share that stand out. Specifically, there are five indicators of a successful coach. They:

- Connect with individual athletes
- Build programs that turn out leaders year after year
- Grow as leaders
- Affect their communities
- Develop a philosophy of coaching that guides them

Every coach in this book is successful, to some extent, in each of the five indicators; however, each *excels* in at least one. This book tells the stories of coaches who excel in each of these five indicators.

High school coaches will certainly enjoy learning about how their colleagues succeed in each of these indicators. As a group, coaches figured out a long time ago that learning from others and applying those lessons to their own program is the quickest path to making everyone better.

Not just coaches can stand to learn, though. The approaches these coaches use to connect with young adults and run successful programs has applications for anyone who works regularly with this age group:

teachers, faith community leaders, social workers, police officers, community center leaders and employers, just to name a few.

As you read these stories, it's important to remember that these approaches aren't blueprints for success. Coaching is, after all, as much art as it is science. Rather, these approaches reflect the way that each of these coaches faced the situation they inherited and then combined imagination, a selfless commitment to their athletes and a strong internal compass (or centeredness), to build something great.

It All Begins with Relationships

I began coaching football a few years ago and vividly recall the first day of practice. Walking back to the locker room in 90-plus-degree heat after a three-hour August practice, I turned to one of my fellow coaches and asked, "What's the key to being successful at this?" Without hesitation, he replied, "Build relationships with your players."

Little did I know at that moment just how expansive the concept of "relationships" would be. Part I of this book is all about how coaches build these relationships—deep relationships that transcend the moments we live in.

Building these deep relationships is not easy in a world where we spend less time together in the public square. This phenomenon was carefully chronicled in the book *Bowling Alone*, by Robert Putnam. Published in 2000, this work chronicled how Americans were drawing ever more into their own worlds and abandoning the civic groups that have long been the backbone of society. The widespread adoption of social media has only exacerbated what Putnam first saw and described.

Marvin Nash, a football coach in Texas, has exerted considerable energy into building these deeper relationships. Simply put, he says that he gets to know every kid "by name and by need." For Nash, this concept applies to both athletes and non-athletes alike. His journey to realizing this will make you smile and move you to tears, as will the other four coaches detailed in the first section who, like Nash, have figured out how to build relationships that last long after a kid's playing days are done.

Multiplying Impact

Connecting with players is tough. Creating a program that connects with dozens of players (or more), year in and year out, is a whole other level of difficult. Part II takes a deep dive into the stories of coaches who've built programs that have known success year after year, while at the same time reaching far more students than those who play on a team.

Such is the case with Barry Wortman, a basketball coach at Blackman High School in Tennessee. Wortman has built a program that touches nearly everyone at the school in some innovative ways—and that's quite an accomplishment, considering that basketball teams are capped at about 15 players in most states.

Wortman's mantra is that they are "chasing success, not wins." That success is grounded in the way that Wortman has managed to include nearly everyone at Blackman: teachers, administrators, school workers, students who want to play but can't make the cut, and students who have no interest in the game. It's an accomplishment that stretches the imagination and stresses the creativity that the coaches in this book bring to their jobs.

The five additional coaches in this section have stories that are no less inspiring. Each offers food for thought about how to break down the barriers that keep so many from benefitting from the things that athletics have to offer.

Growing Coaches and Leaders

Anyone who works with high school age students knows that it's important to continue to develop your own skills and insights.

In Part III, we look at coaches who have managed to continue to get better throughout their career. How they do this varies a great deal: For some, a change in life awoke them to new and better ways to approach coaching; for others, it was learning from their own failures. Still others grew by allowing their students to teach them.

If there's a common thread that runs through their stories, it's this: humility.

For Stacey Swinea, a softball coach in Tennessee, personal growth really began when she came to realize that, sometimes, "it just doesn't mean as much to them as it does to you."

Humility is a concept we are often loathe to accept. Whether you are coaching a high school softball team, leading a team of employees or managing a multinational corporation, displaying humility can be difficult. Most leaders don't want to appear weak or indecisive.

As these coaches show, though, humility is not weakness. Humility is the gyroscope that keeps us balanced, regardless of the turns and dips we encounter in life.

A Broader World

In Part IV, we examine how coaches manage to affect not just their athletes and schools, but the communities they live in. None of the coaches profiled in this book set out to do this; rather, they grew into these roles as the need to do so presented itself.

Shone Evans, a football coach near Galveston, Texas, quickly learned that getting involved with the community came with the job of head coach. La Marque High School, where Evans coaches, is in a community that faces more than its fair share of problems. Just surviving there is a challenge, and Evans literally has to fight for his kids: fight against the gangs always waiting to recruit them; fight against the lack of information about healthy eating; fight against the poverty that has a death grip on his players and school. "When the good guys stop letting you play with them," he says, "the bad guys have a field day."

In little ways. Every day. Evans is helping to rebuild his community in Le Marque through football, and through strengthening the civil society his players need to grow into their futures.

Evans' story, like the others in the section, reminds us that when working with youth, it's critical to look not just at your organization and your relations, but out into the broader world—the place where these young adults will move into, once school is done.

Developing a Coaching Philosophy

Part V highlights the ways that coaches have come to develop a guiding philosophy for their work. As this section shows, there are as many ways to coach as there are coaches. Finding your niche and instilling values is central to success.

Gail Maundrell coaches gymnastics at Turpin High School in Ohio. This sport is highly competitive, but Maundrell found it important to work with her athletes in a way that many coaches in this sport do not. "If you just take off some of the pressure," she says, "sometimes things happen easier because somebody believes in you."

Every coach in this section has developed a philosophical approach to their work that they turn to, time and again. Each coach's approach came about in several steps, after they took a hard look at the situation they were in and "got real" about what was possible. They then wedded this reality to what was possible—what they could and couldn't do in order to move their athletes toward higher goals. Finally, these coaches consistently returned to their approach and continued to refine it.

Pouring In

The stories that follow are inspiring and emotional, full of practical advice and profound wisdom, and overall, are endlessly fascinating.

What they won't do is explain in a neat package why coaches are so successful in working with high school-age students. That's because when dealing with people—and especially young, maturing people—there is no one formula for success.

It's less about what you teach someone than how much of yourself you're willing to pour into a person. That's the concept that Maurice Henriques, another coach you'll meet in this book, applies in his work with young people. What he tells his athletes' parents about his program is probably the best roadmap for youth success that I've come across. "If you're coming here just to get a coach," he tells parents, "this is the wrong spot. If you want a coach who's going to pour themselves into your kid, this is the right place."

Enjoy the stories that follow. Let these coaches' experiences and insights inspire you. Then take their experience, combine it with your own imagination, selflessness and centeredness, and return to your communities—and "pour into" the young adults in your life.

Part I:
Coaches and Their Players

"I get to know every kid by name and by need."
—Marvin Nash

Marvin Nash

"I get to know every kid by name and by need."

Football

Offensive coordinator: San Marcos High School (2020–present)

In football, the head coach sets a program's direction and gets most of the press—good and bad—but it's the many assistant coaches who spend the greatest amount of time with individual players. Marvin Nash has yet to be a head coach at the high school level, but he is an up-and-coming force in Texas football. At San Marcos High School, Nash is the offensive coordinator and also the recruiting coordinator. Here, Nash discusses his relationships with players: the expectations that he sets, his game-day demeanor, how these relationships have formed him as a coach, and the great challenge that lay before his generation of coaches.

Coaching football was not Marvin Nash's first career choice. Shortly after graduating from Austin College, he took a job in the mortgage industry with a burgeoning company out of Dallas called Countrywide. He had a six-figure salary, a bright future, and stability—a powerful combination for a young man who watched his mother battle cancer during most of his high school years and whose father was not around.

When the mortgage industry crashed in 2007, though, Nash's job came down with it.

Rather than regroup and find a similar position elsewhere, Nash called a friend to see about getting into coaching. He took a job coaching a middle-school team.

"We were awful," Nash recalls. "Didn't win a game, and we only scored one touchdown." None of that seemed to matter, though. He connected with those young men—many of whom still are in contact with him today. Nash had found his calling: coaching at the middle and high school levels.

Over the years, Nash has come to appreciate that a coach's voice is the most powerful tool he has. The coach's voice affects players, parents, fans and the community at large. Nash has worked to consistently refine his, and to use it "for good"—in every walk of life.

Just what is the key to finding that voice? According to Nash, it lies in giving yourself fully to relationships with those who trust you to lead them.

Finding His Voice

Recently, Coach Nash was at a restaurant with his family when a busboy stopped to say hello.

"Coach," the young man said, "I don't want to interrupt your time with your family, but I wanted to say 'thank you' for all you did. You changed my life, and I'm not where I am without you."

Where this young man was is in his final year of medical school and bussing tables to make some money. He never played for Coach Nash; he wasn't even an athlete. In fact, as a kid in middle school, he was small and had a tough time fitting in. Yet Nash came alongside him and became a friend. As a football coach, Nash's friendship carried a great deal of weight in the school. The young man had found, in this friendship, someone who made him feel welcome. Nash had helped him gain equilibrium and fit in.

Even with all of the years between the young man's time in class and his meeting Nash in the restaurant, Coach Nash remembered the young man's name: Clayton.

"Physical education coaching allowed me to bridge the gap with him," Nash said. This experience helped to reinforce just how potent a force for good a coach can be, whether interacting with players or with those who aren't.

Not all of the stories in Nash's coaching life have been as happy, however. These stories, as much as any others, have shaped his approach to relating to student athletes—as well as the students he teaches.

By Name and by Need

During Nash's second year of coaching middle-school football, there was a young man who wanted to be part of the team but couldn't be. This young man had cancer. He was, however, an ardent fan. He was in the stands during every game, cheering on Nash and his team. He often adorned a hat bearing an emblem of his favorite college team, the Texas Longhorns.

This young man's name was Colin. As the season wore on his condition deteriorated, and he was unable to attend the final few games of the season. The team ended up playing in the championship game, and when they ended the pregame prayer, they broke the huddle by yelling "Colin!" The team went on to win the game, and though Colin couldn't be there, his mother was there for him. The team gave her the championship trophy.

"That was everything for me," Nash said. "To be part of a group of guys who care." Colin passed away just a few weeks later, but he remains a constant reminder for Nash—a reminder to appreciate every moment, and a reminder that relationships can't be put on hold because you never know when they'll be taken away.

Nash endured another loss several years later—one that was harder in many ways. Nash had gotten to know a young man who was talented in both football and baseball. To all appearances and to everyone who knew him, the young man was living a very good, idyllic high school life. Unfortunately, the young man took his own life. That loss haunts Nash still.

"It made me think that we didn't take the time to ask [what was going on]," Nash says. "We didn't take the time to find out."

Survivor's guilt is a natural reaction to any tragic loss. Many never recover from it, but instead learn to move forward. Nash does not want to forget, saying, "I still think about that young man."

Nash has come to deal with the loss and guilt by changing the way he approaches working with his young athletes. Ever since, he says, "I have made it a point to get to know every kid by name and by need."

Unapologetically Myself

To get to know kids well enough to know their needs, Nash has learned that he must be "unapologetically myself." "Myself" is quite the spectacle on Friday Nights.

Nash, by his own admission, can "go nuts" during games. Lots of football coaches do, of course: coaches can get animated when things go wrong. Nash, on the other hand, starts jumping and yelling and hugging when his players finally do something on the field that they've struggled to master and get right.

And when they mess up?

"I'm calm," he says. "It's my time to teach."

New players are usually a bit confused by Nash's reactions. But soon, he says, they begin to feed off of him. "If I put [my] energy into being positive," he says, "it builds the momentum. Kids thrive off of that."

3.0

Nash's players also thrive off of the energy that he brings to academics. Like all coaches, Nash has seen players with college-level talent get left behind because they couldn't gain admission to a university. When Nash first started coaching, the National Collegiate Athletic Association (NCAA) required a 2.0 grade-point average to be eligible to play at the collegiate level. (The bar is now 2.3.) Many players aspire to just do the minimum, Nash notes, but that isn't high enough a GPA to gain admission into many schools—Division I or otherwise—even if you are an athletic stud.

So, as a young position coach, Nash started requiring all of his players to have a 3.0 GPA in order to play. It was a hard pill for the players to swallow, at first. Yet they responded. When he became an offensive coordinator at Seguin High School, Nash set that same bar for all offensive players. Before long the head coach bought in, and every player was required to have a 3.0 in order to play. For the most part, the players meet the standard—and they do so because they know that Nash has their best interest at heart.

The Next Wave of Hurt

For all of the important things that Nash does, he sees a great challenge facing those in his profession; he also sees a great opportunity for the powerful voice coaches have.

Social upheaval around issues of race are "the next wave of hurt that a lot of kids are going to feel," he says. "It's imperative," he continues, "to use our voices as coaches for positive change."

Nash knows how hard this is going to be.

"Growing up in Texas and the South, it's different," he says. "There are some voices that are heard loud and clear, and some are silent." Nash understands that people are often afraid to speak out for fear of losing their jobs. "But right is right and wrong is wrong. And we want kids to see that modeled."

Nash knows that many people are not prepared to have those conversations that need to be held. It doesn't matter. The time is here, Nash says, and "you have to stand up against wrong wherever it's happening. We have to be that voice of reason."

In what he has already accomplished, and in how he sees the challenges before him, this much is clear: Nash has found his voice. It is clear and focused. It stands on a solid moral foundation. If there is a case to be made for the power of high school coaching, Marvin Nash is the textbook study.

2

Al Fracassa,
from Dave Yarema

"Don't show off."

Football

Head coach: Royal Oak Shrine Football (1960–1968), Brother Rice High School (1969–2013)

When I first started working on this book, a friend in Michigan recommended that I talk with Al Fracassa—a legendary football coach in Detroit and, as I would learn, an influencer who affected the game at every level. My excitement to interview Fracassa was quickly dampened, however, as he kindly and gently (but firmly) refused to talk about himself. Instead, he asked that his players speak for him. His humility, I would come to appreciate, is genuine. Fracassa gave everything to his players, and in turn they remain fiercely loyal and deeply appreciative of him. Indeed, I have come to see Fracassa as the high school coach's coach. Perhaps I'm biased—I love football, and I coach the game myself. Yet there is no mistaking the transcendent effect this man has had not only on his players, but on the entire Brother Rice High School community.

In this, the first of three chapters that relate to Coach Fracassa, Dave Yarema discusses how Fracassa nourished relationships with his players— even long after they had left.

Today, Yarema is known for his career at Michigan State University, where he set a number of passing records in his years as the Spartan's quarterback. He credits much of his success to Fracassa. Yarema learned humility from his high school coach, and later in life, he learned the importance of lifting up others—a lesson he also learned from Coach Fracassa—following a crushing loss to the Iowa Hawkeyes.

When Dave Yarema entered his freshman year at Brother Rice High School, he likely had dreams of winning state titles and earning a college football scholarship. By the end of high school, he had gotten both wishes. Yarema won a state title at Brother Rice in 1980 and went on to be the starting quarterback for the Spartans of Michigan State University.

It's what he didn't dream about getting, however, that has shaped him forever: lessons in how to live a life of humility and honor, from coach Al Fracassa.

When Yarema arrived at Brother Rice High School in 1979, Fracassa was not yet a legend—but he was well on his way. Fracassa began coaching at Brother Rice in 1969 and promptly tallied the most wins in a single season in the school's history. He didn't lose often after that, either. His teams from 1969 through 1978 were a combined 72-12-2, claimed one state title, and sent players to big-name universities like Notre Dame.

Fracassa ended his career with 430 victories and nine state titles. He was a four-time winner of the Michigan Coach of the Year Award, a one-time winner of National Coach of the Year honors, and in 1997 was named the NFL High School Coach of the Year.

That type of success neither interests nor defines Fracassa, though. And he would not let his players fall into the trap of letting the outward signs of success define them, either.

"Don't be a big shot." That's what Yarema remembers his coach both telling him and modeling for him throughout his playing career. More than a mantra, it's at the very heart of who Coach Fracassa was then—and is still, today. It infiltrated every aspect of the Brother Rice football program during Fracassa's 44 years as head coach.

At its core, this expression extols the virtues of humility. Don't brag on yourself, and don't show up your competitors. Like many of Fracassa's former players, Yarema recalls a chilly ritual that helped drive home the point that no one was above the team—or anyone else, for that matter.

After the season had ended, Fracassa required his players to attend practice every Tuesday and Thursday at 6:30 a.m. in the dead of Michigan's winter season, for "agility drills." Yarema recalls them as "really, really difficult," although that may be something of an understatement, as Fracassa learned the drills from no less a task master than the legendary Green Bay Packers coach Vince Lombardi.

If the winter workouts weren't enough to keep an ego in check, the way Fracassa taught his players to handle themselves on game days was. "We came out real quiet before a game," Yarema recalls. "Silent calisthenics. No one yelled and screamed."

Once a game was on, of course, Fracassa did everything in his power to win—though not in a way that would embarrass the opposition. As soon as the lead was secure, the starters were taken out and the backups were put on the field.

As one former player recalls, getting pulled from a game became a matter of pride for the first-string players because it allowed fellow teammates who were not starters to enjoy the fruits of their labor, too. Mike Coughlin, who played for Coach Fracassa in the early 1970s, was—by his own admission—a "third- or fourth-string" player. "But Coach was always pulling for the underdog," said Coughlin. "Always celebrating the scout team and the work we did."

Such training kept players humble when they were together as a team, but Fracassa also ensured that those lessons carried over into the community at large.

"When we left campus or travelled to watch a competitor's game, we never wore a Brother Rice shirt," Yarema said. In the eyes of Fracassa, showing up at a competitor's school with your school name emblazoned all over your clothing was akin to bragging—or worse, trying to show someone up.

Yarema never did wear a Brother Rice shirt while there as a student athlete. And he never wore a Michigan State shirt while playing for the Spartans.

"I couldn't wear it," he said, "because I didn't want to let him down."

Picking Up Others

Not showing people up is just one side of not being a big shot, of course; lifting up others when they're down is the other. Coach Fracassa, not being one to ever stop teaching, modeled that, too—even years after Yarema left Brother Rice High School for Michigan State University.

While at Michigan State, Yarema enjoyed a lot of success. In 1986, fresh off a victory over Notre Dame and ranked 17th in the nation, he and the Spartans hosted Hayden Frye's Iowa Hawkeyes on national television. With less than two minutes to play and trailing by three, Yarema had his team inside Iowa's 5-yard line.

On first and goal, Yarema took the snap, rolled right, and then threw an interception that ended the rally.

Fans can be hard on players about such seminal moments, and their memories can be long. Even today, Yarema still hears about that play from time to time, and the internet doesn't make it any easier to forget. (Google "Dave Yarema," and a video of that play is among the first things that pops up.)

When asked how what he learned at Brother Rice helped him through that period, Yarema says that it wasn't the lessons he'd learned from Coach Fracassa that he leaned on in those days. Instead, it was Fracassa himself who gave Yarema a hand up.

"Coach has written me letters throughout my life," Yarema says. "I have a box filled with them. Handwritten." The day after that game, Fracassa sat down and penned his former quarterback another letter—one that remains one of Yarema's favorites. In it, Fracassa referred to Teddy Roosevelt's *The Man in the Arena* speech. He reminded the young Yarema, "Guys in life who are afraid to fail never do anything."

Don't Be a Big Shot

The lessons taught by Fracassa apply whether someone is on top or at his lowest point in life, Yarema says. "If you interviewed 100 guys, you'd get the same stuff. It all goes back to treating people right. Don't be a big shot."

It all sounds so easy. Yet the fact that Fracassa's former players still celebrate this way of living life speaks to just how difficult it really is.

3

Dana McWilliams

*"You need to take what you do seriously, because
you're really affecting their lives."*

Basketball

Head coach: Upperman High School (1994–present)

When it comes to connecting with athletes, many coaches have to learn how to do it the hard way. Dana McWilliams got a helping hand from her school's football coach, who encouraged her to literally throw away what she planned, and simplify. This practice gave her a lot of flexibility when relating with athletes—flexibility she would need on March 3, 2020.

For Coach Dana McWilliams, the X's and O's of basketball have always been easy.

In fact, they're standard dinner-fare chatter at the McWilliams' home: Dana has been the head women's basketball coach at Upperman High School since graduating from Tennessee Tech (where she played basketball from 1991–1993), and her husband is the men's basketball coach. Together they have four boys, two of whom serve as assistant coaches on the women's team.

Often, people so entrenched in chalk talk remember virtually every moment of their playing and coaching career; that's not the case with Coach Dana. Reflecting on her own time playing at Upperman, she says, "I don't even remember the basketball part all that much."

What McWilliams *does* remember is her coach, Wayne Shanks—and, specifically, the work ethic he instilled in her and the discussions that he had with his players. Talks about life. Talks about the challenges that lay ahead. Talks about succeeding at more than basketball.

What McWilliams did not know at the time was how significant those lessons would prove to be. It all came home to her one night, on March 3, 2020.

Learning the Value of Relationships

Coach Shanks had a straightforward approach with his players: "We're going to outwork people, present ourselves the right way, and look our best," McWilliams remembers him saying. Adds McWilliams, "It all made … sense to me."

When she first started coaching, McWilliams wanted to ensure that her athletes adhered to what she had learned from her own coach. So McWilliams did what any smart, organized person would do: She started making lists of rules.

The school's football coach, on the other hand, had a simpler philosophy about working with high school athletes—and strongly encouraged McWilliams to think differently.

"The football coach saw me writing a bunch of rules," she recalls, "and he said [to] throw it in the trash." Instead, this coach believed in putting the onus on the athletes. "Tell them to do the right thing, and when they don't, deal with it," the coach told McWilliams.

McWilliams seized that advice, and then took it a step further. "Be on time," she tells her athletes. "Be a good student. Be willing to work hard." And as for practice? "I don't have a rule for missing practice because we don't miss practice," she says.

This comical anecdote exposes a central truth that McWilliams has come to appreciate: When it comes to setting standards and connecting with young athletes, "you can't fake caring for them," she says.

Lists of rules, in short, won't cut it.

Caring for athletes is something that happens organically—intuitively, even—in McWilliams' case. So it isn't surprising that, while many high school coaches chafe at having their players join travel leagues or take part in so-called "showcase events," McWilliams works to make sure her girls are seen there. "That's where they're going to get recruited," she says, "and my job is to get them as much exposure as possible."

For the less athletically gifted girls, McWilliams is no less committed. These girls may not be going to college as athletes, but the lessons they learn while playing the game give them the core skills they need to find other paths and be successful.

"You get a kid who has low self-confidence, and then becomes an all-state kid. Or just a confident kid. That's the most satisfying [thing]," McWilliams says.

Often, McWilliams' players pay her back by returning to the school and paying her a visit.

"It's funny, the things that they remember," McWilliams says. She recalls a former Upperman player who went on to play Division I basketball, who mentioned, on a return visit, "Do you remember when you told me ...?"

"I didn't remember," McWilliams admits. "That was a 'wow' moment."

It also made a deep impression on her.

"You've got to be careful what you say, because those words stick with them."

That moment, however, pales to the insight she recently gained into how her girls really feel about her.

Tuesday, March 3

Monday, March 2 was a big day for the Upperman women's basketball team.

The team was set to play for a regional championship. It was a normal day in every way: school, pregame jitters, the game itself. By the end of the day, the team also had an Upperman victory.

When Dana got home that day, she and her husband heard about some storms. Later, they lost power. It was nothing unusual, though: Springtime thunderstorms in the South are notoriously violent, and losing power is a fairly common occurrence.

At 1 a.m., Dana's son came upstairs and told her that one of her players, Ashland, had called. Emotionally distraught, Ashland was determined to find out if Dana was all right. The McWilliams family was, indeed, fine. Ashland was not.

Ashland's home had been badly damaged, and the homes of two other players on the Upperman men's and women's teams had been completely obliterated by a tornado.

Dana and her husband rushed to the scenes of devastation, found out that their players were all right, and called to check on the others. Fortunately, none of the players had been injured.

March 3, 2020 was supposed to have been another game day. Instead, it was a day for taking stock and deciding what to do. Both teams had playoff games scheduled for Thursday; the girls voted to play.

The girls lost that game, but the Tennessee playoff format gives schools the opportunity to play their way back in. On that Saturday night, Dana's Upperman Bees pulled out an overtime 44-42 victory. The next night, the men's team won, too. By the very same score.

Through that chaotic week, it wasn't the heartwarming story of victory that stuck with Dana McWilliams. Instead, it's what her player did. Five minutes after the tornado blew through her player's home, that young woman was on the phone with her coach, making sure that she was all right.

"To think that I was on her mind the very first thing," Coach McWilliams said. "She knew I would come."

It's true: You can't fake caring for your players. McWilliams was reminded just how much that this statement is true in the aftermath of a deadly tornado. "You need to take what you do seriously," she says, "because you're really affecting their lives."

The players at Upperman know that when it comes to their lives, Dana McWilliams will do her level best to affect them for the better.

4

Clarence Lewis

"You know what's right and what's wrong. They know. You just have to let them know on a constant basis."

Football, track and field

Head coach: JL Mann High School (track) (1998–2008), Riverside High School (track) (2017–2018)

Assistant coach: JL Mann High School (football) (1995–2011), Riverside High School (football) (2012–2018), Riverside High School (track) (2012–2016), Greenville High School (track, football) (2018–present)

Discipline is key to successful coaching; so is empathy. Few coaches are able to combine these two as well as Clarence Lewis, who takes us inside just two of thousands of relationships he's developed over the years. What stands out in both of these stories is not just the sacrifices on his part that these relationships required, but the vulnerability of the students who most needed him. Lewis helps us better understand how to keep a healthy balance between the two.

Clarence Lewis is the son of a third-grade teacher and a Southern Baptist minister. His mother gifted him with a heart for those on the margins and for those who struggled. She never gave up on a student. His father gifted him with a powerful voice and the passion of a religious convert. He set up the guard rails and expected people to stay within them.

Since 1995, Lewis has made use of both of his parents' teachings on the high school athletic fields of South Carolina.

Discipline is front and center, something that Lewis learned from his own high school football coach, Jim Fraser. "He taught me what coaching was really all about," Lewis says. "He was a stern disciplinarian."

Fraser is a legend at T.L. Hanna High School in South Carolina's Upstate region. Now retired from coaching, he was recently honored by having the school's football field named after him.

Lewis' track and field teams have won a string of state and regional championships—testimony to the power of discipline in molding high school athletes. Discipline alone, however, doesn't get the job done.

"Touching the lives of our athletes was the key for us," Lewis says. He and his coaches weren't just interested in "what can you do for me on the track, but how I can serve you to be the very best that you can be."

The Investments

All coaches invest time—a lot of it—in working with players. Lewis' investments, however, go far above what is expected.

Fabian Davis and Lana Heslop are two cases in point. Their high school years are separated by more than a decade, and their athletic careers went in very different directions. Coach Lewis' steady hand is the tie that binds them together.

Davis was a natural athlete, successful in whatever sport he tried. His home life, on the other hand, was a place of struggle. Davis recalls it as "not the best." Lewis recalls a home led by a single mother who had trouble with boyfriends.

As he was single at the time, Lewis opened his home to Davis.

"He became a great mentor to me," Davis said. "He would tell me, 'Whatever I have, you have.'"

On weekends, Davis and Lewis would watch North Carolina basketball together. They would also talk about the importance of school.

"He wasn't a fantastic student," Lewis says. "I think because of all the stuff that was going on at home. So he struggled a little bit academically. We had to really push to get him eligible."

Lewis would harp on grades, but it just didn't register with Davis. It took college coaches walking away from him to make Davis realize that he had to focus and get it done in the classroom.

"Everything sports-wise came easy for me. My problem was keeping my focus on the things that I needed to do," Davis said.

With Lewis' guiding hand, Davis stayed focused and earned a football scholarship to Wake Forest University. Old habits die hard, though, and he soon found himself on academic probation.

Lewis was there.

Davis would come home from school and stay with his former coach. Lewis would mentor him about school and get him back on track. Davis went on to have a stellar career with the Demon Deacons, then played a few years in the NFL. By then, his ability to focus at all times was no longer a problem. In fact, it was that very focus that earned him a spot on the roster of the Tampa Bay Buccaneers.

"Coach John Gruden gave us a playbook that was about 6 inches thick. … I had to learn that playbook in seven days. … I never missed a meeting. Was never late," says Davis. His persistence—and focus—paid off.

While at summer camp, Davis was consistently asked to run a pattern right at the safety. The ball never came to him. It's easy, in those moments, to lose focus: To forget to the do the little things, such as check over a shoulder for the ball. It's not coming anyway, right?

One practice, Davis ran that same pattern for what felt like the thousandth time. He looked over his shoulder—and this time, the ball was in the air.

"They were trying to overthrow me," Davis says. He turned on the jets and made the grab. "That catch was my little stint into the league."

The Phoenix

Lana Heslop was a rising star at Riverside High School. She had started out as a soccer player, but was burned out after years of playing. During her freshman year, Heslop reluctantly transferred to track because her parents had a strict rule that she must play a sport. It took a while, but she came to embrace the sport—and Lewis was a big part of that.

"He made me feel like I mattered to my team," Heslop recalls. "It made me feel invincible, like I could do anything."

In fact, Lewis made all members of the track team feel that way.

"He was known around the team as 'the second father,'" Heslop said.

During her sophomore year, Lewis named Heslop co-captain of the sprinters. As she matured on the track, school records began to fall. During her junior year, however, Heslop began to struggle physically. She noticed that her legs wouldn't always do what she wanted them to do. During one meet, she was on pace to beat her own record when, 20 meters from the finish line, her hip partially dislocated.

As she rehabbed, Lewis was there every step of the way. His support was invaluable, she says, even as doctors were baffled by the physical ailments. She spent time in the hospital and was wheelchair-bound at times.

"It was a very disorienting period," she said.

The students around Heslop didn't help, either.

"High school is so inter-ripping," she says. "People play the telephone game, spread wild rumors. I had no self-esteem. No sense of self-worth."

Coach Lewis would not let go, though. He had Heslop continue to serve as a team captain and play the role of a mini-coach. These small acts kept her going. "Coach Lewis was never upset about me having to miss practice to do physical therapy," she says. "Very accommodating of everyone's situation. Very lenient in more extreme situations. He knew us. Knew our character."

In time, Heslop recovered and was looking forward to a great senior season.

It never materialized.

Heslop inexplicably started losing clumps of hair like a cancer patient on chemotherapy. She developed mouth ulcers and red spots on her skin. She felt constantly fatigued. Nauseous. She would take naps before practice and meets, and her blood vessels would break when she ran. Doctors ran a battery of tests, trying to figure out the mystery illness. Then, just before a regional meet, Heslop got the news: She had two forms of lupus.

That ended her track career. She emerged an even more powerful young woman, though, and what Lewis showed Heslop during those years forever shaped her character.

"He made me a lot more empathetic toward other people. Made me want to listen to others' stories," she says.

Heslop is doing that today in Lexington, Kentucky, where she's a student at the University of Kentucky in medical laboratory sciences and a volunteer with Operation Making a Change. There, she mentors and works with at-risk children.

Says Heslop, "I'm very happy with where everything led."

I'm Hard on Them, but I Love Them

According to Lewis, "Billy Graham once said a coach will impact 1,000 more lives than the average person does. Everyone doesn't get that chance, but we do, and I don't take that lightly."

It would be surprising if Lewis has only touched 1,000 lives in his 25 years of coaching. Heslop and Davis aren't anomalies: In my interviews with them, both would jump on tangents about other athletes they knew whom Coach Lewis had gone to the same extremes for. Sometimes further.

Lewis sees himself as just giving the kids what they want.

"I believe kids want discipline. You know what's right and what's wrong. They know. You just have to let them know on a constant basis," he says.

It's that last line that best explains the impact Lewis has had over the years. It's the lesson his mother modeled: discipline is great, but you have to be there for everyone and never give up. Lewis certainly knows this.

"We have been successful because of what we invested in them."

5

Nathan Yates

"We're not leaving until you tell me what's wrong."

Football

Head coach: Riverbend High School (2019–present)

I am on Coach Yates' staff at Riverbend High School. As an assistant, I am a coaching neophyte with a little knowledge about the kicking game and a passion for helping young people become their very best—both as football players and as young adults. Early on in my coaching stint, I asked Yates what it takes to become a good coach. He offered a single-word response: "relationships." As the conversation evolved, he shared this story. In a number of important ways, it set me on the journey of writing this book.

Coaching demands a careful balance between pushing people further than they think they can go and developing a listening, sympathetic ear for players. Push players too hard, and they won't listen to you; become too close a friend, and you lose the ability to challenge them and their effort.

How far one can push players varies. One of the more extreme examples involves the legendary Alabama coach, Paul "Bear" Bryant. Before taking a coaching job in Tuscaloosa, Bryant coached at Texas A&M University. Bryant's first football camp was held in Junction, a small town in the Texas Hill Country. That summer, in the grip of a drought, Junction became the ninth level of hell for the men who arrived. Of the roughly 100 players who left A&M for camp, just 35 survived the 10 days and 10-hour practices to return and play football for the Aggies.

If any coach tried that today, they'd have no job and the school would have a mountain of lawsuits. Bryant could get away with it in 1954. A big reason is the relationship he had with his players.

As one of the so-called Junction Boys, Dennis Goehring had this to say about the experience to Tommy Deas of the *BamaInsider* in 2013: "I look at it like this: There's a junction in everybody's life. ... It comes in different forms. This was a junction that took us in the right direction with an attitude that was positive. Once we got back, we knew we were going to have a winning team—there wasn't any question about that."

Demanding, Listening

Nathan Yates doesn't operate junction-style practices, but he *is* demanding. He's also a master of knowing the right time to push and the right time to listen. He's honed this talent over more than 15 years of coaching, and though I have seen his mastery of this tightrope act at Riverbend High School, it's an episode he shares from his time as a defensive coach at Massaponax High School—a longtime central Virginia powerhouse—that best demonstrates his abilities.

Yates built a stifling defense at Massaponax. It's true that he had talent to work with: more than a few of his players, over the years, went on to play in college. But not every kid on his teams was a five-star recruit. Indeed, most of them were like one of his young linebackers. Physically imposing he was not, but he bought into a program, as well as an approach, that favored disciplined, hard workers over gifted athletes who weren't committed to their teammates.

At practice one day, a usually focused linebacker simply wasn't concentrating. Yates got on him, as good coaches will, and tried to motivate him to give his best. But as the practice wore on, it became apparent that the young athlete just wasn't performing that day.

"What's wrong with you today?" Yates asked. "Is something going on?" He asked several versions of this question for a half-hour.

Finally, Yates asked one of his fellow coaches to take over and pulled aside the struggling young man. Putting his hands on his shoulders, Yates looked in his eyes and said, point-blank, "We're not leaving until you tell me what's wrong."

The young athlete could hardly look his coach in the eyes.

"It's my mother," he said. "I just learned that she has stage 4 pancreatic cancer."

At that, Yates grabbed the young man, bear-hugging him, and held him while he cried in his coach's arms. "We're going to get through this together," Yates told his linebacker.

Active Listening

Life pushes all of us to the breaking point. Coaches, in particular, see this more acutely and with more regularity than many others do. A coach's job is to push young men and women to their breaking point, and then push them to go further and do more than they ever thought possible.

The expression "How are you doing?" is a passive statement, and it has become almost flippant in our society. We say it or hear it a hundred times a day. And we've all lied by answering, "I'm good, and you?" when we really aren't. Similarly, we've all suspected that others we greet are doing the same.

We're all busy. We all harbor private struggles. And we all have some sense for when others are struggling.

How many of us, though, will take precious time out of our day to transition from a passive tone—"How are you doing?"—to a more active approach—"You're not leaving until you tell me what's wrong"?

That's coaching at its finest.

Part II:
Coaches and
Building Programs

"You've got to be who you are, and that has to match
and work well with where you are."
—Bobby Alston

6

Barry Wortman

"We're chasing success, not wins."

Basketball

Head coach: Blackman High School (2011–present)

Assistant coach: Morehead State University (2006–2010)

Winning consistently at the high school level is tough. If you define "success" by the number of wins and losses your team garners, you may be setting yourself up for a frustrating ride. Barry Wortman defines success differently.

Attend a junior varsity basketball game at Blackman High School on a given night, and you may well witness Coach Barry Wortman serving as the JV assistant coach. Holding a clipboard. Tracking timeouts. Helping with substitutions. That's what assistant coaches do, with the hope of one day becoming a head coach and allowing others to deal with these important details. Nothing unusual about that, except for this: Wortman is the head coach of the men's varsity basketball program.

Wortman—and all of his coaches—rotate roles, because Wortman knows that there are no unimportant jobs. In addition, rotating roles is the most effective way Wortman knows to build relationships with his players. And those relationships are the foundation for what he is trying to create on and off the court: success.

Casting a Wide Net

Wortman doesn't field teams laden with superior talent; rather, he fields teams that get the absolute most out of the talent they have. Blackman High School men's basketball team has made the sectional tournament each year that Wortman has been in charge, and it's made the state tournament 7 out of 10 years. Yet, only three of his players have gone on to Division I programs. His 2016 team was ranked in the national top 20 by *USA Today*, yet no one from that team went on to a Division I program.

To find the players who can play in his system, Coach Wortman casts a wide net.

"Our program's not for everyone," he says, "but we try and keep as many ninth and 10th graders as we can who are willing to buy in to what we're doing."

Some years, that means running more than one team for the ninth graders—all the more reason, in Wortman's mind, to be involved at both the freshman and JV level.

"When players come from your freshman team, to your JV team, to the varsity team, you have good relationships with your kids," says Wortman. "So the sooner you're building those relationships with your players, the better."

Ultimately, the varsity basketball team can only carry so many players. That means at the end of spring practice in a student's sophomore year, the coaching staff has to make some hard decisions about who is moving to varsity and who is moving on to something else.

While those decisions are never easy, Wortman knows that telling a kid and his parents to "keep working" isn't the answer. The kids who don't make the team can be involved in other ways: as statisticians, or with the student-coaching program. Other students move on to track, drama, or another area in the school where they can grow.

Wortman wants his kids to reach their full potential, whether it's on the basketball court or in another area of school life. He believes that being involved with the basketball program as a freshman and sophomore instills in students some basic concepts that serve them well, wherever they end up.

HAT and 4EO

Every player who enters Wortman's program has to "buy into," embrace and live the program's two mantras.

The first is HAT:

H—Humble
A—Appreciative
T—Thankful

HAT is something the coaches and teams practice, and don't just recite.

"We try to get outside ourselves and thank the people who make it all possible," Wortman says. "Be appreciative and thankful, instead of taking it for granted."

Every week, Wortman's players thank their teachers for their work. The team has made both the custodial staff and cafeteria workers part of the program, too, so coaches and players are expected to regularly express their gratitude for everything these folks do to make the program happen.

"Everybody has value in our program—even the guy filming the practices and games," Wortman says.

The second mantra is 4EO: "For Each Other." It's about accountability to the team, and to one another.

If someone is down about their playing time, Wortman expects his guys to support their teammate. If it's snowing and someone needs a ride to practice, they're to be there for each other.

Don't expect to see a bunch of shirts around school with "HAT" or "4EO" emblazoned on them, though.

"We don't want a logo on a shirt," says Wortman. "We want to live it."

The End Goal

Wortman knows what it is to win. As an assistant basketball coach at Morehead State University, he was part of a team that garnered a win in the 2009 National Collegiate Athletic Association (NCAA) Tournament; as head coach at Blackman, he's won a state title.

Coach Wortman will tell you that wins are not what matters, though. "We're chasing success, not wins," he says.

Success boils down to the goal that Wortman sets for every team he coaches. "We want to play in the last game of the year—or cry."

It's not unusual for teams to cry when a season ends. This behavior can be seen every year at the end of the NCAA Tournament, when CBS cues up *One Shining Moment* and images of teams jumping for joy after winning, or lying on the floor and crying after losing, flash across TV screens. It's probably safe to assume that most team members who are crying are doing so because losing hurts. That, though, is not the kind of crying that Wortman preaches about.

Wortman talks about the tears that get shed when the journey comes to an end: when the relationships you've worked so hard to develop and nurture over four years—a group of players that has come together—must now move in new directions. It is at that point when you realize that the bond that brought the team members together—basketball—is ending.

Wortman points back to the 2016 state quarter-final game as a great example. They lost to eventual state champion Memphis East. "There were about 3 minutes left, we were down by 13 or 14, and we knew it was over. I called a TO, and we cried in that time out; we cried on the bench for those last 3 minutes; we cried in locker room after game. We cried the next day when we met."

That pain, says Wortman, "came from being unbelievably connected as a team."

"The pain of that loss was real, but the deeper pain came from knowing that many on that unit would never again be together as a team," says Wortman. "That hurt was so special to me. It showed how much the program and the staff and the players all meant to each other."

That feeling of hurt was as special to Wortman as the elation he felt following his two state titles and his win in the NCAA Tournament.

That's success. And for as long as he's coaching, that's what Wortman will continue to chase.

7

Fernando Gonzalez

"Wrestling gives these girls a purity of knowing who they are,
and understanding themselves, and having a purpose."

Wrestling

Head coach: San Fernando High School (2002–present)

Women's wrestling is surging in popularity. States that 10 years ago would never have considered allowing girls to compete in this sport are now finding themselves in the awkward position of justifying why they won't let women participate. Fernando Gonzalez knows the feeling. Fresh out of college and new to coaching, Gonzalez had to confront his own doubts about women as wrestlers. It didn't take him long to get on board with this idea, though.

Here, we follow Gonzalez's growth and learn how he confronted this sea-change at San Fernando High School to build a powerhouse program.

Fernando Gonzalez has been involved with wrestling most of his life. He competed in high school and continued to participate in this ancient combat sport on the club team at the University of California, Berkeley. So when he started teaching at San Fernando High School after college, it was no surprise to see him back on the mats, coaching.

He was taken back a bit, however, when young women started showing up for the team. Not many—somewhere between two and five a season between 2002 and 2013—but enough that he had to quickly figure out how to coach wrestling in a co-ed environment.

At first, it was easy. Gonzalez was an assistant coach and just followed the lead of the head coach, whose mindset was pretty straightforward. "Wrestling is wrestling," the head coach told Gonzalez. So Gonzalez kept his focus on the sport, and not the gender of the person doing it.

Head Coaching Job

In 2002, Gonzalez was named the wrestling head coach at San Fernando High School. The women not only continued showing up, but they began showing out, too.

"The opposition—when they had to wrestle our girls, they didn't quite know what to do," Gonzalez said. "The girls took it to them, and it just kind of grew."

The wrestling part was easy; it was the other challenges he faced as head coach that were more difficult.

"I developed this father-figure complex," Gonzalez said. "I have to protect the girls from the boys, so I was always kind of cognizant of the situation; you want to make sure the boys aren't inappropriately touching or taking advantage of the situation."

Because he was clear about what was expected, there were few interpersonal problems between the guys and the girls. The girls, however, were getting the short end of the competition stick.

The boys' team was powerful. Prior to 2013, the boys' team was always in competition for the sectional championship and, in fact, has won 17 sectional championships.

"When it came down to finals—qualifications for the California Interscholastic Federation (CIF), and state—the boys were usually the representatives for the weight class," Gonzalez said. "The girls wound up on the second team. The boys always won the wrestle-offs and represented the team."

Reverse

While the boys were the stars prior to 2013, girls were making their presence known. So much so, in fact, that there were unsanctioned state championships for girl wrestlers. In 2009, Sarah Saenz won an unsanctioned championship. Her success brought a lot of attention to the success his girls were having.

When, in 2013, California finally sanctioned the sport for girls, Gonzalez remembers that the trickle of women wanting to wrestle turned into a flood. Rather than four or five young women showing up, suddenly there were 30 women who wanted to be involved.

The community really got behind the young women, too.

"San Fernando High School is majority Hispanic," Gonzalez says, adding that the area is very "community-oriented." Says Gonzalez, "Many of the students that we have have parents and grandparents who went to school here."

Coach Gonzalez notes that, while parents whose boys wrestled were more inclined to drop them off at school and ask what time they should return to pick them up, the girls' parents would travel to the meets—which usually last all day—and lend support.

The team responded.

In 2017, Adelina Parra became the first San Fernando High School girls' team wrestler to place first in the state in her weight class. The girls' team won first place in the state championship in 2019 and took second place in 2020.

Along the way, the SFHS girls' wrestling team has won no less than six Los Angeles City Section championships.

Building Character

Today, women's wrestling is surging. A 2019 story in *The Wall Street Journal* reports that girls' participation in wrestling has quadrupled in the past decade, while boys' participation has declined some 7%. According to Gonzalez, the explanation for the growth isn't all that hard to understand.

Wrestling, unlike any other sport, helps its participants to find balance. It's the ultimate expression of yin and yang.

The training is brutal, Gonzalez says, and participants have to keep their weight at a certain level, and "then you have to square off against another human being who has gone through the same thing that you did," he says. "So there's a level of mutual respect that emerges."

With respect present, matches are about avoiding mental mistakes and getting oneself out of position, Gonzalez adds.

"Everyone knows the moves," he says. "At the junior level, it's about who's going to outmuscle who. But at the upper tier, it's about who's going to get into position, wait and anticipate, and explode into the move that you're going to do."

Wrestling is all about proving oneself. That's all the motivation anyone needs to do it, too—boy or girl.

Says Gonzalez, "Wrestling gives these girls a purity of knowing who they are, and understanding themselves, and having a purpose."

Transitioning

Gonzalez continues to coach both the boys' and girls' teams at San Fernando High School. The school has finally been able to create a separate training facility for the girls. Currently, Gonzalez is looking for the individuals who will continue the program.

Naturally, he's looking within the community. He has alumni from his girls' teams coming back and working as assistants. His hope is to turn the program over to one of them, just as his mentor turned the program over to him in 2002.

The next generation of girls' wrestling coaches at SFHS won't face the same challenges Gonzalez faced; they will, however, face others.

When they hit those bumpy waters, they need only to look back at their mentor and remember the lesson he took from his head coach, about how to deal with the bumpy waters of change: "Wrestling is wrestling."

8

Maurice Henriques

"I'm always looking for that moment to say the right thing."

Track and field

Head coach: Niwot High School (2010–present)

Founder: REAL Training

Coaching is a slogan-rich business. Every team has them. Every coach has their pet sayings that they come back to over and over again. One of the more commonly used slogans is, "Change the culture." The meaning of this slogan is clear to athletes and coaches: In order to win, we must change the way we do things. What doesn't get spoken about is how this gets done. In this chapter, Maurice Henriques explains how he accomplished change at Niwot High School. He also provides a key to success necessary for anyone wanting to "change the culture."

Fans of college football will always remember 1994 for the Miracle at Michigan. That's when the University of Colorado's Kordell Stewart heaved a last-second, 64-yard Hail Mary pass to Michael Westbrook to beat the Wolverines.

Maurice Henriques will always remember that year, too.

Henriques was a member of that Colorado team, but on the last play of spring ball before the season started, he wrecked his shoulder and had his season with the Buffalos ended.

"I was so low," Henriques recalls, "because I didn't have football."

Just before that memorable game at the University of Michigan, Colorado's head coach, Bill McCartney—a master motivator—called Henriques into his office. He sat down his defensive standout and said to him, "when I rank my players on character, you are in my top five."

For Henriques, it was the right thing to hear at the right time.

Now, more than 25 years later, Coach Mo—as Henriques is known around Niwot High School, just outside of Boulder—has built a track and field powerhouse, all based around finding the right thing to say.

Changing the Culture:
A Tired Expression Made New

Listening to Henriques is an inspiring exercise, and one can't help but feel better about himself after spending time with him. He's a gifted storyteller, with a life story that will motivate you to overcome whatever struggles you face. He's also great with expressions. In fact, they roll off his tongue with the fluidity of Usain Bolt exploding out the blocks.

That Henriques can motivate with words is hardly noteworthy—after all, inspirational stories and quips are in the toolkit of every coach. What sets him apart is the depth of learning that is behind his expressions.

When he took the job as head coach of track and field at Niwot High School, Henriques inherited a team and a coaching staff that had known little success over the years.

"I met with all the assistants, laid out a plan, and we just started building," he recalls. "It was tough. We had to change the culture."

There is probably no more tired an expression in coaching than "change the culture." Asked what that meant, Henriques had to stop and think for a moment. Then he began listing everything he did. Perhaps the most obvious is what he did at first.

"I showed up," Henriques said. "At times, there would only be three kids." But he was there, and they worked.

This behavior signaled to the kids that Henriques' first concern was them—however many of "them" there were. When Henriques hired coaches, he made sure that they were people who followed suit: They had to love the sport and love the kids.

"At the end of the day," Henriques says, "kids don't care what you know or did; just that you care about them."

Another measure that Henriques took was insisting that everyone wear the same clothing at practice and at meets.

"Everyone had to wear black pants and the Niwot hoodie," he said. "A coach told me, 'There's no way that is going to happen.' Now the kids love to get the hoodie. It's a pride thing. It makes them part of something."

When kids tested Henriques, they weren't allowed onto the bus for meets.

On meet days, everyone stayed to the bitter end. More than just getting his athletes to stay, Henriques got them to take pride in standing together for the final race, the 4 x 400 relay.

"It's the last race, you're tired, [and] it's all about heart," says Henriques, noting that the coaches and the kids all stand, cheer on and urge their teammates. "It's *our* race," he says.

There are rites of passage involved when joining the team, too.

"When a kid throws up for the first time after a hard workout, they get a T-shirt," says Henriques. It marks the transition from joining the team to being a part of the team.

Each year, Henriques also employs a "word of the year," and he begins every season by talking about that word. It's the rallying cry for the year. Practices, too, are tightly scripted. "We start on time, we end on time," he says.

To end the tensions between track runners and cross-country runners, Henriques makes each run the other's routines. That exercise typically ends any talk of one group working less hard than another. Henriques also sets the warmup groups during practices, intentionally splitting up friends and cliques to ensure that the focus is on the team and not on any one individual.

He also chooses the captains. They aren't usually—or even often—the best athletes; they're the best teammates.

At the end of the year, everyone leaves the team banquet with something because, Henriques says, "everyone is a part of it." If the team wins the state title, the school pays to put every athlete's name on the trophy.

As the list of culture-changing actions winds down, Henriques laughs, saying that he didn't realize how much there was to it. And therein lies the key to his success.

Henriques' words and actions are synchronous: The two cannot exist independently, in his coaching or in his life. This fact was made evident long before he even got to Niwot.

I'm a Work in Progress

Before Henriques was "Coach Mo," he served as a juvenile intensive probation officer for 18 years. To help the troubled youth he worked with, Henriques started a program called "Jocks." Each member of Jocks was given a T-shirt with an expression screened on the back: "I'm a work in progress."

Henriques understands, on a deeply personal level, what that expression means—and what embracing it can do for young people.

"I'm really big on positive stuff. If you get that negative thought, it will bring you down," he says. Henriques has witnessed this effect far too often both in his own life and in the lives of the kids he has worked with.

A dedication to setting kids on a positive path also explains why, when talking with Henriques, state titles and championships (and the numbers of kids he's coached who've gone on to collegiate and professional careers) almost never come up in the discussion.

"I enjoy the process," he says.

In the years that Henriques' team wins the state title, he's back at work the next day, coming up with the word for the upcoming season. "The kids start asking right away what the word's going to be," he says. Belief is central to Henriques' process, too.

"My whole life has been about getting people to believe in something," he says. "The goal is to show up and work, and then we'll see what comes up."

Pouring In

Most would marvel at what Coach Henriques has accomplished at Niwot, but several years ago, he went looking for additional opportunities.

In 2007, Henriques founded a track and field club for youth called REAL Training. Since its launch, he has beaten the same steady drumbeat with the kids who come, with their parents, and with the coaches in the program. "Running is just a very small part of it," he says.

Given the founder's name and reputation, families often join the program in hopes that their kid will turn into the next track star; Henriques stops that discussion at the beginning. "I tell parents, 'If you're coming here just to get a coach, this is the wrong spot. If you want a coach who's going to pour themselves into your kid, this is the right place.'"

This doesn't mean that the kids don't work, though. Henriques trains his young athletes as hard as he trains those at Niwot. On the days that he brings his athletes from Niwot High School to his club practices, the high school athletes are "blown away by the talent these kids have," he says.

To ensure that the focus stays on "loving up" the kids in his charge, Henriques will not talk to parents in regard to the sport. He will, however, talk with them if they need help in any other area of their child's life.

Henriques has found that parents—almost by nature—don't care about the team. "Parents only care about their kid," he says, "and there's absolutely nothing wrong with that. Parents are there to bring snacks, drop you off, pick you up, and cheer you on at meets." If that sounds a bit harsh, consider this: Henriques' athletes' parents "don't complain," he says, "because they know the standard." Parents also know that Henriques is concerned, first and foremost, with their child's development as a person.

Attitude and Effort: That's What I Look For

The notion of pouring love into kids is what Henriques has been about his whole life. There's a risk associated with doing this, of course: You're likely going to be hurt along the way. As author E.A. Bucchianeri wrote in *Brushstrokes of a Gadfly*, "when all is said and done, grief is the price we pay for love."

Yet the successes are worth the price of pouring in.

Of the many success stories that Henriques shared with me, one sticks out. In it, a young woman at Fairview High School—where Henriques coached before going to Niwot—was routinely asked, along with her fellow athletes, to write down her goals. She wrote, simply: "I want to be an astronaut." Today, Jessica Watkins is living that dream.

"I'm always looking for that moment to say the right thing," Henriques likes to say. Every bit as important are the words that he gives his athletes the freedom to express.

What "Coach Mo" is really teaching, after all, is how to bind one's words and actions to create an unstoppable force in life.

9

Bobby Alston

"You've got to be who you are, and that has to match and work well with where you are."

Football

Head coach: Memphis University School (1997–present)

One of the decisions every leader struggles with is determining how much control to give to those being led. For 25 years, Coach Bobby Alston has set hard boundaries for his players—but within those boundaries, players have considerable latitude to chart the team's season. He does this because there is a lot expected of his players, and not just on the field. The majority of the players at Memphis University School come from families who can afford the tuition. Often, these families are leaders in business, in the community and across the world. Alston sees his job as much about living up to players' expectations as about winning on the field. After all, leadership—like winning—is learned.

At Memphis University School, it all begins with "the roadmap."

Each January, Coach Bobby Alston meets with his seniors at a lunch and goes through the cornerstone of the MUS football program: the roadmap. This document spells out exactly what the program is about, defines each person's role and explains how success is determined. While Alston allows each year's seniors to set the road signs, the map remains the same season after season—as it has for more than 25 years.

There's a reason for Alston's unyielding approach to the game, but it has little to do with football. "We coach kids who have been given a lot of gifts," he says, "and we are not going to let them waste those."

To ensure that they don't waste their gifts, Coach Alston keeps his players relentlessly focused on who they are as a team. Often, that is best summed up in the roadmap:

Good, better, best
Let it never rest
Till our good is better
And our better, best.

Good, Better, Best ...

Memphis University School is an elite, all-boys day school serving students in grades 7-12. Its alumni include the CEO of FedEx, Fred Smith, and the founder of AutoZone, Pitt Hyde. When it comes to finances, the school wants for little.

The majority of MUS students start life in a better place than most other young people: in stable, well-to-do homes and with all of the economic and social perks that come with that. Over the past 15-20 years the school has worked to diversify its student body, yet even these diverse students often start in a good place.

Of an incoming class of 100 ninth graders, about 20 will be from families that are much lower on the socioeconomic scale. What these young people lack in money, though, they more than make up for in academic aptitude. These students are fully capable of handling the school's demanding academic regimen.

Having gifts does not always mean that one's life is easy, however, and it's the struggles that tend to meld together Alston's teams.

"I have kids from the extreme ends of the economic system, but when you get them in the locker room, they have the same issues," says Alston. "The kid who has everything may have a father who is never there, so he shares something in common with the kid whose father isn't in the home."

This isn't to say that issues don't arise between players from radically divergent economic classes, but finding common ground in their struggles puts them on the course to being the best that they can be.

Let It Never Rest

If finding common ground in their personal struggles helps the athletes relate, it's the power of competition that drives them forward. The same is true of the coaches.

"You're in coaching because it's a calling," says Alston. "There's a higher purpose than winning games."

There is an irony here, however.

"If you don't win games," Alston says, "you're not going to have a job very long, and kids aren't going to listen to the message."

Alston has had plenty of success, and plenty of kids are listening. The Upper School (grades 9-12) has about 450 students, and of those, nearly one-third are involved in football.

Part of the reason for the interest in football, according to Alston, is that MUS is in the South—a region where football is still a big deal and people want to play. Beyond that, the coaching staff and the most athletically gifted players make sure that the less-talented athletes are valued. "They're not just dummy holders," Alston says.

Another thing that motivates students to join the team is how the Owls practice.

"We've always practiced like a pro team practices," says Alston. "We don't have a lot of physical contact. We don't put a small kid against a five-star athlete. The great players also understand that part of their job is to make those other kids feel loved and respected."

Till Our Good Is Better

Bonding and embracing competition are but two pieces of many in building a team. The most difficult—and most time-consuming—piece is keeping the players "on an even keel," says Alston.

The coach notes that, "You're on a journey with a team." Like in any journey, there are smooth stretches, rough patches over broken pavement, and even the occasional flat tire. The key is to control your response when things aren't going well.

Alston stresses to his players that "when we don't have a good day on the field, or have a problem in the locker room, that's life—and you have to deal with it."

How a problem is dealt with is what makes the difference. Keeping composure, understanding the right and wrong ways to address a problem, and learning to compromise and learn—these are the keys to success.

Part of the roadmap is also dedicated to handling victory.

"It's not only how you handle the losses," says Alston, "but also how you handle the wins."

Typically, the team puts each of its opponents into one of three categories:

1. **Games MUS should win, because they have superior talent.** In these, respecting the opponent is key: Do not let them hang around and gain confidence.

2. **Toss-up games, because the talent pool on each team is equal.** These games define a team, because most often, the team with the most character will win.

3. **Games in which MUS is the underdog, because the opponent has superior talent.** In these, the team must love the challenge and raise its level the entire week of the game, in order to earn a chance to win.

There's also a fourth category: no guarantees. Players must recognize that football, like life, involves a certain amount of luck or fate that individuals can't control. Sometimes, even when you do everything right, you lose. How you respond to that adversity is the best test of any team.

And Our Better, Best

When all of this comes together, Alston's players build a community and friendships that last a lifetime—which circles back to the irony of character-building and winning writ large. After all, the two are inter-twined: As Alston attests, you can't have one without the other.

"As coaches, sometimes we forget that not only are we calling plays and figuring out schemes, we're trying to build a community that allows posi-tive relationships to develop," says Alston.

With more than 25 years of coaching at MUS under his belt, Alston has been around long enough to see the fruits of binding character to winning. But even before he knew success, he embraced these ideals.

Alston's players will tell you that he doesn't give motivational speeches. "We are not a rah-rah program," he says. Alston's pregame talks usually go something like this:

> Guys, you've worked hard for this moment. If we go out and do what we're supposed to do, there's a chance we'll win the game. All the emotions are going to be gone the first time you get hit. From that point forward, it's about executing fundamentals and standing next to the guy next to you when things get tough.

Alston and his team don't need a rah-rah spirit. No, they have some-thing better.

A roadmap.

10

Adam Priefer

"A good team chemistry is like having an additional Division I player on your team."

Basketball

Head coach: Oakwood High School (2001–2002), Centerville High School (2003–present)

When coaches talk about "team," they usually are describing a group of people committed to common goals. People who share a lot of mutual trust. Most often, it's the coach's reputation and knowledge of the game that is the glue that holds a team together. Adam Priefer has taken the concept of team in a different direction. He didn't have that depth of knowledge or a reputation when he started coaching, so he had to create an environment that valued learning; out of that, he built team chemistry. Today, Priefer's reputation is solid and his knowledge of the game is unparalleled. His girls' basketball program at Centerville High School in Ohio is routinely considered not only one of the best in the state, but in the nation. The success, however, has not changed how he builds "team." It all starts, still, with a culture of learning.

There was nothing in Adam Priefer's youth that would lead one to think he'd make his name as a girls' basketball coach—and certainly not at a competitive level. He didn't even play the sport much growing up.

Priefer comes from a football family. His cousin Mike Priefer is the special-teams coordinator for the Cleveland Browns, and his uncle Chuck Priefer enjoyed a long history in both major-college football and the NFL.

Everything changed when Adam was 19 years old, and his sister asked him to help coach her team at Altar High School in Dayton, Ohio. He was a student at the University of Dayton at the time, and though he knew next to nothing about the game, he agreed as a favor to his sister.

That was in 1996—and Coach Priefer has never looked back. How does one go from volunteering with his sister's girls' basketball team to creating a powerhouse program at Centerville High School? The answer lies not in what Priefer has learned, nor what he gives to his players. It is in the environment of learning he creates, which elevates the concept of "team" to a whole other level.

Learning Lab

It's certainly true that, over 24 years, Coach Priefer has become deeply knowledgeable about the X's and O's of basketball. Entering the profession *without* that knowledge, however, had a profound effect on how he approaches building a program. In fact, to think of Priefer primarily as a "coach" is to gloss over what's truly distinctive about his program at Centerville High School. Priefer entered the game as a student, and in many ways, he has never *stopped* being a student.

"If you become a sponge and listen and learn, and always work to learn more, that is the key," he says. "If I make a mistake, I admit that to the kids, and I expect them to do the same."

In short, Priefer's program is more akin to a 24/7 learning lab than a traditional high school basketball team, for which the coach sets the agenda and gets the athletes to buy in. In Priefer's system, everyone is responsible for learning more about the game, their teammates, and how to pull together as a team.

Priefer's learning lab is driven by three goals, which are shared by everyone:

1. Building the athletes' confidence
2. Increasing everyone's basketball IQ
3. Creating a team that is truly owned by everyone involved

Special Up

When Coach Priefer first started coaching, the one thing he saw most among the players he worked with was a lack of faith in themselves. It's a problem that many of his young athletes still face.

"Our first job is to make these kids as confident as we can," he says.

Priefer has taken several steps to help his athletes with their confidence. One such step was getting his athletes involved with Special Olympics—a natural connection, as Priefer's father has a longstanding relationship with Special Olympics and his entire family was involved while Priefer was growing up.

What the young women see when they get involved in Special Olympics is both the sheer joy the athletes experience while competing and the outpouring of support.

"I think we take for granted, at times, the number of people who support us," says Priefer. Watching how the crowd gets behind those athletes reminds Priefer's players that the fans are also there for them and play an important part in motivating them. This, in turn, helps build the girls' confidence.

Priefer and his staff also use practice to build confidence. Priefer believes that a key part of his job is finding the drills that will create opportunities in practice, so that his players can ultimately enjoy success. If a player is struggling with crossover dribbles, they'll run drills that will teach the skill and ensure it can be done effectively. If a player is struggling with shooting, they'll run practice rotations so that players gets good looks and a better chance to convert their shots.

It all comes back to learning: figuring out where struggles are, then creating an environment in which athletes gain skills instead of worry about being weeded out because they're struggling.

Another path to self-confidence is happening organically, and not just at Priefer's school. Girls' basketball in general has become more competitive over the years, and girls are increasingly playing ball with boys during open gym and on playground courts. The results are better skills and a greater confidence in the girls' abilities. Ten years ago, Priefer notes, this kind of interaction did not happen.

Training the Next Generation

As Priefer's players grow in confidence, he also makes sure that they improve their basketball IQ. Each summer for the past 16 years, Priefer has had the older girls on the team coach the summer junior high league. There are a number of advantages.

From Priefer's perspective, this interaction is a great way for the seventh and eighth grade girls to learn what to expect when they arrive at Centerville High School. His players are often better equipped for this task than the coaches, he feels, because the junior high girls already look up to the older girls. Both groups relate to each other as growing young women, too. The seniors know well what the young girls are going through, both physically and emotionally. The junior high athletes find, in the seniors, markers of success they can look to and knowledge of who will carry them through difficult times.

Perhaps more important is that the experience of coaching junior high athletes in the summer league helps Priefer's more-senior players better appreciate coaching. By leading the summer leagues, they get firsthand experience in seeing what Priefer and his staff see on game nights at Centerville. This gives his players a greater appreciation for what the coaches are trying to accomplish, and it increases their trust in the coaches. After all, nothing builds empathy quicker than having to step into someone else's role.

Team Mesh

The final element in Preifer's approach to coaching is the meshing of his players into a team. Building confidence, raising players' basketball IQs: any athlete needs confidence and knowledge to perform at a higher level. To mesh the players into a team, however, requires a building of team chemistry.

To bring it all together, Priefer does not cut breaks for anyone. On the day we spoke he had had his players out running, in preparation for the season ahead.

"When we work out, everyone comes," he says. "Freshmen through seniors. Our best player today ran every inch that our freshman kids were made to run. We try and teach them all the same way."

Priefer knows that the team is meshing when he hears the younger players questioning why things are done a certain way, and the older players responding with seven simple words: "This is the way we do it." Priefer calls this "one of my proudest moments as a coach."

The admonition comes from the players, not the coaches. The focus is on "we," and not on how "the seniors" want it done, or the coaches telling their athletes how it's done. The 2018 team is one that Priefer points to as one that worked this teambuilding formula to near perfection.

The 2018 team wasn't expected to accomplish much. It was a younger team, with just three seniors, and the top scorers on the team were a freshman and a sophomore. On some teams, this would create resentment. Not at Centerville.

"The three seniors were fine with not being the leading scorers," says Priefer. "They took the leading role in how practices would run and how games would be won."

Every player on that team had a role and embraced her role, putting self second to team. This happened because of the connections the girls had made in the summer junior high league and at Special Olympic events. It happened because the entire team trained together, with no one person being asked to do more or less than another.

That team finished 25-3. It lost in the regional finals to the eventual state champion.

"This is what can happen," Priefer says, "when you have great chemistry."

This is what team in a 24/7 learning lab looks like.

Andrew Hyslop

"No one owns the player."

Soccer

Co-executive director, coach: Carolina Elite Soccer Academy (CESA)

The landscape of high school sports has undergone a seismic shift in the past 20 years, with "club" (or "travel") teams rivaling high schools for players. Today, colleges recruit directly from these leagues, and many athletes feel they must choose between playing for their school and playing for a club. Not surprisingly, tensions between high schools and clubs can run high.

Andrew Hyslop has had a front-row seat to this evolving sporting scene. He is co-founder of Carolina Elite Soccer Academy, an organization in the upstate region of South Carolina with 3,500 athletes ranging in ages from 4 to 18. He has worked to open dialogues with and support high school coaches, as well as to empower young athletes to speak for themselves and advocate for what they want and need.

Growing up in a military family, Larissa Heslop moved a lot.

"Soccer was the one constant in my life," she says, noting that the game provided a dependable, comfortable, safe space. "If I was on the field, nothing else going on in life mattered."

The game was a part of Heslop's life through high school and college. She earned an athletic scholarship to Eastern Kentucky University (EKU) and, in 2020, was one of the athletes nominated for the National Collegiate

Athletic Association (NCAA) Women's Athlete of the Year award. (This award recognizes athletic achievement as well as academic and leadership achievements.)

Her life, however, hasn't just been all about soccer, all the time. "It was never a goal of mine to play in college," she said. "It all just progressed."

Kids Who Love the Game

Heslop's description of her relationship with soccer and her progression through the ranks is precisely the experience that Andrew Hyslop would wish for every athlete. (The two individuals are not related, despite the similarity in their last names, but they are connected.) Hyslop coached Larissa through her years playing for Carolina Elite Soccer Academy, or CESA, in South Carolina. He also played a key role in getting her recruited by EKU.

Ideally, Coach Hyslop says, a soccer player's career—whether it lasts a year or a lifetime—will unfold at its own pace.

"You want kids who grow into players who love to play the game," he says.

In his 30 years with CESA, Hyslop has become increasingly concerned that coaches, parents and supporting organizations are professionalizing the game. Everyone, it seems, wants to lay claim to a piece of an athlete. And when they have that piece, many feel it gives them the right to control the athlete.

This, Hyslop says, is the challenge that coaches today must own up to and begin to change.

Tug-of-War

When authority figures see an athlete as someone who they have a piece of, young athletes find themselves being the proverbial rope in a tug-of-war between coaches and other authority figures in their lives. Many young soccer players feel this tension most directly when their club and school seasons overlap: After all, club soccer programs compete year-round and high school soccer in South Carolina is traditionally played in the spring, with playoffs starting in late April.

When these seasons overlap, coaches often give their athletes a choice: Play for me, or play for them. This forced decision occurs, Hyslop argues, because coaches feel that they partially "own" the player. He suggests a reset for all authority figures in a student athlete's life. Everyone, he contends, needs to begin with an understanding that "no one owns the player."

Hyslop's suggested mindset requires a rethinking of the coach-player relationship: seeing a young person not as a soccer player, but as a young person who plays soccer. That slight shift in perception, he says, changes everything.

"The key for me," says Hyslop, "becomes understanding the right mix of academic, social, soccer and personal for each athlete."

When you approach coaching the game as Coach Hyslop does, the clash over schedules plays out a bit differently.

"Kids want to play for their school teams," he says. "The beauty of high school is, whoever lives in your area goes to that school." He reasons that kids naturally want to play with the people they grew up with, as well as play against their neighboring friends.

To help his student athletes navigate the do-I-play-high-school-or-club choice, Hyslop has taken several steps. The first step involves proving to CESA athletes that he respects their desire to play for a school team.

"We show up to watch high school games," he says. "Being in there, crossing the line to enter the stadium and watch the game, matters." It shows, he contends, that a coach values their choice.

To some local high school coaches, the second step that Hyslop takes matters even more. Knowing that high school playoffs begin in late April in South Carolina, CESA shuts down for a period of time in order to allow its athletes to compete on their school teams.

Several high school coaches in the region appreciate the step, and they and CESA have developed a good working relationship. Other coaches remain leery and keep their distance.

Regardless of the reactions, Hyslop is sending a broader message to high school coaches and parents: "We all have a part in changing the narrative."

Maturing

Coach Hyslop doesn't pretend that his relatively modest steps will resolve all of the tensions between high school teams and club teams. While he has accommodated his players by creating a way for them to play on their high school teams during the playoffs, there are also compromises that he is not willing to make. For example, he continues to train and play athletes in the spring.

It's also true that there can come a time, for some athletes who play for CESA, when some hard choices have to be made. For example: Do I play in this high school game, or do I attend this club tournament out of town, where there will be 300 college coaches in attendance? (It's worth noting that very few of CESA's kids will have this decision to make. Of the 3,500 in the program, only about 200 play at the elite level and have a legitimate shot of playing in college.)

Most of CESA's athletes play because they enjoy the game and because CESA gives them an arena to play in throughout their high school years—even if they don't make the high school team. Yet even for those who must make tough decisions, it's all part of growing up. No one can do everything he or she wants to do in life, so, we make choices about the things we most want and pursue those more aggressively. Coach Hyslop's contention is simply that kids are given the room to grow into these decisions.

As kids spend time with CESA, Coach Hyslop says he believes that, athletically, "the kids have a really good idea of where they fit in. When kids begin to realize their ceilings, they then have to figure out how much they want to push through."

In other words, you may be able to play Division I or Division II soccer in college, but are you willing to make sacrifices in the other areas of your life in order to reach that goal?

Certainly, learning to make these types of difficult decisions is hard for the athletes. But it's also hard for coaches and parents. In his years at CESA, Coach Hyslop has seen many athletes with the ability to play at the highest levels of college soccer, but for reasons related to their personal, social or academic lives, they didn't wish to pursue that level of competition. In those instances, authority figures have to respect the decision made.

Communication

Changing the narrative around high school and club sports requires leaders buying in, too. It requires that student athletes learn to speak for themselves and handle the difficult conversations that ensue. This is a lesson that Coach Hyslop wants all of his players to learn, and he presents opportunities both on and off the field in order to learn it.

When a CESA player wants to play for his or her high school or middle school team, coach Hyslop prepares them to have that discussion with the school coaches. He sets CESA's schedule each October, and he expects his players to take that schedule to their school coaches and talk about how they can work together.

And for those who have no desire to play for a school team? Well, they learn to stand up for themselves on the field. Regardless of whether players are in the elite class or playing in the lowest division, Hyslop coaches them hard.

"If you're coaching a mid-range team, we want you to treat the players as if they're a top-range team," he says. "They can still develop. Still improve." This invariably leads to tough conversations.

Larissa Heslop recalls many difficult discussions with Coach Hyslop during her playing days. Ultimately, she came to understand that it's about getting on the same page. "My goal was to express myself, but also understand what he would rather have happen," she says.

That skill has served her well.

"I had to deal with it in college," she says. "And I worked part time in college, so I was able to use those skills with supervisors. I know how to talk to people in a way that brings us to a compromise."

Coming to a compromise is what high school and club coaches need to do. A simple idea—no one owns the player—may well hold the key to getting them there.

Part III:
Coaching Development

"Sometimes it just doesn't mean as much to them as it does to you."
—Stacy Swinea

12

Allison Kinniard

*"When we were losing, losing, losing, we just
kept preaching, 'we are getting better.'"*

Field hockey, softball

Head coach: Lancaster High School (field hockey) (2013–present)

Assistant coach: Lancaster High School (softball) (2008–2016; 2020)

The story of Allison Kinniard is really that of two individuals: Allison, and her athletic director, Pam Bosser.

"Allie," as Allison is known, was tasked with a near-impossible job: rebuilding a field hockey program with few players, inferior facilities and a reputation for being little more than a recreational-quality team. To top it off, she had never played the game and knew very little about it.

In talking about how the program has moved from nearly being cut to one that is rising up the power rankings, Kinniard and Bosser are quick to credit each other. That's fair: After all, these two share a symbiotic relationship that reflects not only the importance of developing and supporting good coaches, but the importance of having women in leadership roles at the high school level.

This story will be told in two parts. In this chapter, Kinniard talks about the challenges associated with rebuilding a program while starting with every conceivable disadvantage. In the next chapter, we'll look at the refreshing perspective that Bosser brings to women's high school sports; how she stood her ground for Kinniard; and how she is creating a model for future female athletic directors to follow.

When Allison Kinniard was asked to take on the field hockey team at Lancaster High School in Ohio, she knew that she had her work cut out for her. The school didn't have a great surface for the team to play and practice on, and most of the girls had little to no experience with the sport. Then there is the economic reality: Lancaster serves a relatively poor part of the state, and many young women there can't afford the high-end equipment that girls in more well-to-do schools can afford.

These were far from Kinniard's only worries, though. Prior to this coaching opportunity, she had never played field hockey in her life and she knew next to nothing about the sport.

Yet athletic director Pam Bosser knew that Kinniard was the right person to bring back the program.

"I wanted someone in there who would raise the expectation that the program could be competitive, and would hold the kids to accountability," says Bosser. "I knew she was the kind of person who would take the time to learn the sport, and she would bring the intangibles. A good coach can coach anything."

'Oh, My God, We Scored a Goal!'

The going was rough early on. The first year, Lancaster had 11 athletes come out for the team. There was no freshman squad; no JV squad. And for those who don't know the sport, a field hockey team has to put 11 players on the field.

On the upside, Kinniard jokingly commented, everyone had the opportunity to play. "I didn't have to deal with parents complaining about playing time!"

The ability to find the good in trying situations has served Kinniard well. Not only did she have just 11 players that first year, but they were players who did not have the skills or the experience to compete with the teams Lancaster faced.

Located in a rural part of Appalachia, the Gales played teams that were mostly in or near the city of Columbus. Many of the rival schools were better financed, and the players the Gales played against came from families that could afford to pay for private coaching and development programs.

The outcome was predictable: Lancaster didn't win a single game under Kinniard's leadership during her first year. It didn't win a game the second year, either. Or the third.

Yet Coach Kinniard was undeterred. She knew that it was going to be an uphill battle, so she focused less on the scoreboard and more on achieving little goals.

"The marker of being good isn't always winning," says Kinniard. "For us, it's more about what we improve upon." To her players, she pointed out, "Look how many goals we scored this year versus last."

At every practice and at every game, Kinniard stressed the little goals: improving individual skills; executing a perfect pass; not turning over the ball; holding the opposing team to two goals in the second half, as opposed to six goals.

Achieving these goals built confidence and gave the players something to build on. Coach Kinniard still remembers one of the initial "big little goals" reached by her team.

"The first time we scored a goal, the look on my girls' faces was, 'Oh my god, we scored a goal!'"

According to Bosser, Coach Kinniard excels at recognizing and then praising the small successes.

"Allie does a great job of setting those little goals," she says. "Then, she really celebrates those."

Gaining Attention

The team wasn't winning, but Kinniard was slowly winning over students. She actively recruited players from her softball team to her field hockey team. She teaches freshman students, so she began to take that opportunity to recruit them to play, too. She got involved with clubs in order to raise her profile—as well as that of her team—within the community. She became involved with the Varsity L Club, and began working football games on Friday nights.

"My involvement in the clubs started to bring the girls in," Kinniard says.

Today, Lancaster has a JV team. Kinniard started a summer camp, and this year's crop of incoming freshmen will be the first to join the program after having gone through Kinniard's learning process. The coach has even gotten some of the girls involved with local travel teams.

The Gales field hockey team still isn't winning a lot—it had 5 wins, 2 ties and 9 losses last season—but it *is* winning, and individual players are beginning to get recognition.

"A couple of years ago, we finally got our first person named honorable mention," Kinniard says. "The next year we got one on second Team. This year we got two on second team and one on first team."

There is still a long way to go, but each year, the Gales are closing the gap on their competition.

"When we were losing, losing, losing," Kinniard says, "we just kept preaching, 'we are getting better. We are improving.'"

These days, the competition does not take this team for granted.

Yet Kinniard sees growth in other ways, as well.

"I like that the players are upset when they don't win," she says. "At the same time, however, they can understand that they want to be better, and we are getting there."

Her just-graduated group of seniors certainly knows this.

"Some of our seniors this year wrote me a letter," Kinniard says, "and they said, 'we'll be back to watch you win games next year!'"

No doubt they'll be back. And there's no doubt that Kinniard will be logging wins.

After all, she holds all the intangibles.

13

Pam Bosser

"The goal is to win, but the purpose is to develop kids—not only physically, but also mentally, socially and emotionally."

Head coach: Lancaster High School (1990-2002)

Athletic director: Lancaster High School (2010-present)

Without Pam Bosser, Allison Kinniard's experience raising up field hockey at Lancaster High School may well have looked very different. In this chapter, Bosser talks about why Kinniard was the person for the job; the importance of understanding both the goals and the purpose of high school sports; and how she is working to create a sporting environment that is not only more equal in how programs are treated, but also in how they're valued.

When Allison Kinniard was mired in a three-year losing streak as head coach of the Lancaster Gales field hockey team, athletic director Pam Bosser was approached by the superintendent, who asked her, "Tell me again why we have a field hockey team?"

In coaching, everyone gets fired eventually. A few lucky coaches leave when they are ready, but most often, that decision gets made for them. Wins and losses often drive that decision. For this reason, the superintendent's question was one that any athletic director would expect to get in the midst of a losing streak. Bosser, however, did not give a typical answer.

"For the same reason we have a baseball team," she said. "The goal is to win, but the purpose is to develop kids—not only physically, but also mentally, socially and emotionally."

Bosser's entire career has been about balancing the goals of coaching with its purpose. She appreciates the importance of precisely balancing the two because, as a woman, she lived through an age when young women had few genuine athletic opportunities—and of the ones they did have, most were looked down upon as second-class programs.

The Power of Sport

When she became the athletic director at Lancaster, Bosser was asked who she looked up to in the world of sports while growing up.

"That was tough," she says, adding that, when she was young, "there weren't visible female athletes to model." Instead, Bosser chose a male: "The athlete I idolized was Pete Rose. Had his poster on my bedroom wall."

Bosser has worked her entire career to ensure that other young women can answer that same question differently. Certainly, things today are better—at least in some respects—than they were when Bosser was growing up. "I had never seen a female in an AD seat when I was playing in high school, and many of my coaches were male," she says.

Today, young girls can admire accomplished athletes like Brandy Chastain, a two-time FIFA World Cup champion and two-time gold-medal Olympic champion. Alternatively, they can find coaches to model: Women like Alyssa Nakken, a baseball coach with the San Francisco Giants, and Katie Sowers, a football coach with the San Francisco 49ers. Bosser understands how important these models can be. Her own worldview opened up when she went to college and, for the first time, saw a female administrator in the assistant athletic director's chair. She also had female coaches on her field hockey team. "It began to open my eyes," she says.

Perhaps the most influential person in the development of Bosser's professional ideals was Catherine Brown—an Ohio University professor, coach, international athlete, field hockey official, member of the 2012 class of the Field Hockey Coaches Hall of Fame, (reluctant) member of the Ohio University Athletic Hall of Fame, and tireless crusader for women's rights. Brown took Bosser under her wing when Bosser was in graduate school and, says Bosser, "helped to mold me and my philosophy about the role of coaches and their influence on the lives of young athletes."

Bosser came away with one undeniable truth: sports matter. More specifically, sports matter in the lives of high school students.

The aforementioned truth is a point that Bosser drives home every year, when the school holds its parents' meeting for the families of student athletes.

"I put up a slide that shows some 88% of male CEOs credit their leadership ability to what they learned in athletics," says Bosser, who notes that this speaks, without a doubt, to the power of sports to grow leaders. When the same question was put to women CEOs, "Ninety-four percent credit their leadership to their athletic careers."

Never Questioned My Decision

Kinniard believes that having a female athletic director has been critical to her success.

"I really took over field hockey because the athletic director asked me to," she said.

Bosser has stood behind her protégé not only because she believes in Kinniard, but because she knows the talents she brings. When asked if she ever doubted her decision to bring on Kinniard as the field hockey coach, her response was quick.

"No. I want people who model character intentionally, create expectations. Allie brings that," says Bosser. "Her personality is energetic, and she expects a lot from her kids."

Bosser expects no less from any of her coaches—male or female. She shows that respect each year, too, when it's time to divvy up program money.

"I don't show any favoritism toward any sport. Yes, football and basketball bring in more money, but I budget according to roster size and need," she says. This, more than anything else, has endeared Bosser to her coaches. Kinniard certainly agrees.

"I feel like, at our school, our AD is really fair about allocating money to all the programs," says Kinniard. "Having an athletic director that is a female, she tries hard to make sure things are fair across all sports."

Still, there's a long way to go before women's sports are seen as the equal of men's sports.

"Do I feel women's sports in general get as much recognition as men's sports?" asked Kinniard. "Absolutely not."

Making It Right

Today, Bosser isn't just working to create an equal playing field for all of the athletes at Lancaster High School; she's also working to right some old wrongs, both because it's the right thing to do and because young women today need to appreciate those who paved the way.

"The second year I took this job, we did some research," Bosser said. "Prior to Title IX in 1972, the players on the girls' teams at LHS weren't considered varsity athletes."

So Bosser brought these women back to Lancaster, and at the halftime of a basketball game, she awarded them their varsity letters.

In the work to elevate women's sports, the past and the present have to work together to build a bridge to a more equal environment for all athletes. Bosser and Kinniard are laying bricks as fast as they can.

14

Rick Huffman

"We created this culture where it's OK to have a face-to-face and tell how they feel about each other."

Soccer

Head coach: Grand Valley High School (2014–present)

In life, it is from our most bitter moments that can come the foundation of our greatest successes. Rick Huffman is a living testament to the power of taking the bad and making something good out of it. From a short-circuited college soccer career, Huffman found the ingredients he needed to develop as a coach and walk alongside his players, as he helped move them from perennial underdogs to feared competitors.

When Rick Huffman accepted the job as soccer coach at Grand Valley High School six years ago, there was nowhere to go but up.

"We were the running joke," he says. "If there was a school that had a young team and wanted to beat someone, they'd call Grand Valley."

Today, though, no one is laughing. It's not just the increasing tallies in the win column that has people's respect, either; it's the culture that Huffman has built.

Coming Alongside

Wins and losses were the last thing on Rick Huffman's mind when the athletic director named him the head soccer coach at Grand Valley High

School. The school sits in a rural part of Ohio, just east of Cleveland, and it's a football school. For many years, the school's soccer program was just an afterthought—something for kids who couldn't make it on the gridiron, a program for misfits.

The athletes Huffman inherited were out of shape, not grounded in soccer skills and suffering a crisis of confidence. The players were down on the team and down on themselves. Before Huffman could lead them, he had to first come alongside them and mentor them.

In a very real sense, Huffman could relate to his players.

A star soccer player in his youth, Huffman was granted an opportunity to play the sport at the collegiate level. Yet just before the season started, he sustained an injury that benched him. His career never got back on track. "I became a very bitter, angry young man," he recalls.

A series of mentors came into his life and helped him right his ship. Years later, Huffman's Grand Valley soccer players needed the same support.

"I told them, 'I will give you insight; I'll partner with you; but, ultimately, you have to make the decision,'" he says.

Huffman's coming alongside student athletes happened on two fronts: the physical and the emotional. On the physical front, Huffman started with the most basic element of soccer: running.

Estimates for how far a player runs during a soccer match can vary by age group and by position. Midfielders, for example, run more than backs and forwards. On average, however, you can expect high school players to cover about 4 or 5 miles in a game. Huffman's first group of players at Grand Valley were in no shape to do that. So he instituted a 1-mile warm-up run and required his players to regularly execute timed 3-mile runs.

At first, the players struggled just to finish. They were covering the 3 miles in 40 minutes—sometimes more. At that pace, the players were moving at little more than a slow jog.

Along with the running, Huffman began drilling the basic skills of the game: ball handling, dribbling, passing and the running of simple sets. These early efforts didn't yield wins, and it didn't take long for the grumbling to start—not so much from the players, but from the parents.

One father took his son and left the team. Another, who was serving as an assistant coach, quit. These individuals didn't understand the focus on conditioning, and they couldn't see how the skills work was helping. As that first winless season dragged on—0 wins, 15 losses, 1 tie—the frustration from the stands only got louder.

Opening Up

The parents weren't happy, but the kids were beginning to buy in. As the din from the parents grew, Huffman saw, in the backlash, an opportunity to begin to build a team.

Huffman launched a book club, requiring his players to read one title as a team. A favorite is *The Hard Hat*, by Jon Gordon, which is a true story of a coach, his team, and how they came together. Team-building exercises followed.

When parents began ripping on their sons' teammates, Huffman developed a role-playing game in which the kids would act out the situations and learn how to respond.

Slowly, these changes began to take hold. Times in the 3-mile run began to fall. Individual skills started to improve. Though Grand Valley kept losing, the games grew tighter.

More importantly, the players began gaining confidence, were becoming more physically fit and were beginning to take pride in their program. They started to hold themselves accountable, which was made possible because Huffman turned the seniority system on its head. At many schools, the freshmen and sophomores are stuck doing the dirty work—cleaning up the field, carrying equipment, lining the fields. Huffman had his seniors take these jobs.

Huffman wanted the seniors to be the models. The servant-leaders.

It took time, but the transformation has come. Younger players will now approach seniors and let them know that they admire them and that they want to be like them. Older players will work with younger players in the classroom and on the field, to help them get what they aren't understanding.

When players make a mistake, they voluntarily own it and then apologize to their teammates—whether the mistake is a poor decision on the pitch or in another area of life.

Following each game, Huffman asks his players to take 24 hours and think about their role in the game. The next day, each player stands in front of everyone and evaluates his own play.

"They're more critical of themselves than we are," says Huffman. "When they first started self-evaluating, they had no idea how to do it. Now they are accountable. This is a game above the shoulders."

Huffman adds, "We created this culture where it's OK to have a face-to-face and tell how they feel about each other."

Finding a Friend

The caring culture created by Huffman has had enormous impact on both the individuals and the team as a whole. The stories roll off of Huffman's lips as rapidly as Lionel Messi turns lost balls into goals. One of Huffman's favorite stories is about a kid who had lost his father and wanted to join the team.

"Are you any good?" Huffman had asked.

Recalls Huffman, "The kid laughed, so I asked what he wanted out of the team. He said, 'I want a friend.' He was never a captain, but we called him the captain." The student athlete, it turned out, suffered from depression, and his family couldn't afford the medications he needed. Coach Huffman asked permission to make some calls on his behalf, and the student got the medicine he needed. Today, that "captain" is working toward an undergraduate degree.

Another student athlete was dealing with his father beating his mother. The one person he could trust was his coach.

"It's all about mentoring, and family, and loyalty," Huffman says.

Goal

The impact that Huffman has had is visible everywhere at Grand Valley. You see it in his kids' work ethic, and the way the school has begun to accept and cheer for the team.

Physically, his players are in the best shape of their lives. That 3-mile run they previously couldn't do in 40 minutes—they're now doing it in 18 minutes. This past year, the team won the most games that it's ever won.

No longer are these players ridiculed, either. Several of the players began kicking for the football team (and have, for a number of years now). This practice has helped to build the bond between players in the two sports, and they're beginning to cheer for one another.

Huffman is far from done, though.

The word is out on Grand Valley, and the team knows that rather than being the unit that pulls the upset, it's becoming the target that teams work harder to beat. Today, Huffman is working to build resiliency in his players, too.

"The boys have to understand now what it is to handle the pressure of being expected to win. That's the maturity piece that we're going to work on moving forward."

The team is learning to handle that pressure. Last season, Grand Valley played its first Division I team. At first, the kids were stunned by both the number of players on the other sideline and the talent they displayed. They took some early shots, but settled down and wound up coming back. They lost by just one goal.

Coach Huffman keeps upping the ante, as well as the compassion he has for each of his athletes.

"I keep all the notes from the kids who are seniors. They talk about being physically fit. Having a passion for fitness. If we can make someone passionate about something, we're all about it."

The toughest thing now? That senior night game.

"You blink," Huffman says, "and it's over."

For one group, yes. Yet it's just starting for the next. And they'll be reaching for even greater heights.

15

Tom Generous

"The key to coaching is to tell a kid that she's getting better."

Squash
Choate Rosemary Hall

When Tom Generous took on the job of girls' varsity squash coach in the early 1970s, he found himself in over his head. Through dedicated study, and an openness to what his young athletes could teach him, Generous found his way. Here, we walk alongside Generous those first difficult years coaching a new sport at a school that places a premium on success in every aspect of life.

While serving with the U.S. Navy in the Philippines, Tom Generous learned of a game not widely known in the United States at the time: squash. Played with a tennis-sized racquet on a court with four walls, it's a fast-paced sport that demands excellent hand-eye coordination, stamina and bursts of speed.

Generous was intrigued by the game—and played it—but his heart was with baseball, a sport he both played and coached. Generous and squash would cross paths years later, though, at an exclusive boarding school in Connecticut called Choate Rosemary Hall. The crossing path of Generous and squash proved serendipitous, even if hardly ideal in the beginning.

Choate Rosemary Hall is comprised of two single-sex schools: Choate for boys, and Rosemary Hall for girls. Generous arrived at the boarding school in the early 1970s, fresh from graduate school at Stanford University. As a faculty member, Generous was expected to not only teach but to coach, as well. He naturally gravitated toward baseball and was the Choate boys' junior varsity coach for over two decades.

One day, Generous was walking with the athletic director's assistant. She was complaining that Rosemary Hall was dropping a sport, and when Generous inquired as to which sport it was, he was told squash—only a year old at Rosemary Hall, at that point.

"The Rosemary Hall teachers don't expect to coach at all," the assistant told him, "and the Choate teachers don't want to coach at Rosemary Hall."

To that, Generous replied, "Did you ask me?"

And he got the job.

The program didn't exactly excel his first year, but Generous received a top-flight education in what it takes to be a great coach of high school students—thanks to a very young Frances Norris, or "Francie."

Francie's Gift

That first season, Generous had to find whomever he could and convince them to play on the team. One of his players was Francie, a ninth grader. Francie was a decent squash player among a group of athletes that wasn't particularly good. Consequently, she ended up ranking third on the team.

When Rosemary Hall would compete against other schools, Generous' young third-ranked athlete was matched against the competitor's third-best player—invariably, someone older, stronger and much more experienced. The results were predictable: a perfect losing season. Francie was 0-12 in matches, and 0-36 in games. (A match is composed of five games; you must win three.)

"I remember one day, I started chewing her out because she wasn't hitting a proper rail shot, and she began to cry," Generous recalls. In that moment, he came to appreciate the fragility of a young athlete's psyche.

"The next time we played," he said, "she comes off the court, and I said, 'Francie, that was an amazing corner shot you hit in the second game.'" Her face brightened, and she nearly squealed, "Oh, did you see it, Doc?" (Generous' athletes often called him "Doc," out of respect for his having a doctorate degree.)

"Indeed I did," he said to Francie, "and I'm so proud of your improvement."

Being a Team

That inaugural season, the Rosemary Hall squash team fared no better than Francie did, losing against every opponent it played. To make matters worse, a fire had destroyed the team's facilities at Rosemary Hall and the team had to play every game on the road. The girls couldn't even practice at school, instead having to travel about 20 minutes to Yale University, to use the courts there.

Road trips are tough, and losing streaks wreak havoc on self-confidence. Combine the two, and you have created a situation that can quickly become debilitating.

Through Francie, Generous came to appreciate the fact that dwelling on the negative is no path to success. He began finding ways to insert some joy and positive learning into the not-so-fun experiences. Generous started by making the team's road trips more enjoyable.

Renowned for academic excellence, students at Rosemary Hall are required to spend substantial time hitting the books. To allow them space to stay on top of their work, Generous required the athletes to spend their first 45 minutes of every trip studying. "After that," he said, "they could fool around and just be kids."

On the court, Generous strengthened his team's bond by showing the girls how to help each other as they grew as athletes. Each player is on her own during a game, but to be effective as a team, fellow athletes have a role to play. "During breaks between games," Generous said, "the players got together and coached one another."

The argument can be made that, because everyone was so inexperienced in the game, it was easier for the players to bond. They were in it together, after all: They would either grow with each other or fall all together.

As Generous recalls, the best part of that year was seeing that the girls "got a lot out of being a team." They would carry with them, throughout their lives, this appreciation for having and being teammates.

The Ray of Hope

Generous held that first team together by adopting a more positive approach to coaching, creating space for his athletes to enjoy their youth, and empowering the girls to grow together as a team.

Like his athletes, Generous had a lot to learn about the game itself, too. That first year, he learned by closely watching his team's opponents and educating himself on the ways to coach the game. "The opponents I paid particular attention to," he recalls, "were the ones who were very good. I didn't know the game, but I'm a pretty bright guy, and when I asked myself, 'What does he/she do?' the answer wasn't long in coming."

One of the answers that came to him had nothing to do with the technical aspects of shot-making, but instead focused on conditioning.

If he couldn't win matches, Generous could get his girls into shape. At the time, too many coaches treated female athletes different than male athletes. Generous would have none of that. He recalls telling a fellow faculty member, "If I treat these kids like girls, they'll play like girls. If I treat them like athletes, they'll play like athletes."

That language may sound askew today, but in the early '70s, it was a bold statement.

Generous put together a vigorous conditioning program with a great amount of stress on running in order to build the cardiovascular system. "They took great pride in their conditioning," he says.

From that first difficult season, it didn't take long to turn things around. By the second year, the team was winning tournaments. By the fourth year, the team was competing against the best teams in the country. By the time that Generous was done, he had coached 47 nationally ranked girls.

Francie Norris ended up being one of the leaders. In fact, Francie was the captain of the 1980 team that won the New England Championship. She then went on to build her life as a teacher. According to Generous, she's spent the majority of her career as an English teacher at the prestigious Harvard-Westlake School in Los Angeles.

Teaching the Teacher

The title "coach," like the title "teacher" or "doctor" or "judge," carries with it the weight of authority—whether the individual who holds the title is knowledgeable or not. As a young coach, Generous did not let that authority get the best of him. He remained a student.

Francie Norris proved an excellent teacher.

16

Stacy Swinea

"Sometimes it just doesn't mean as much to them as it does to you."

Softball

Head coach: Davidson Academy (1993–present)

Part of excelling as a coach is appreciating that the people who play for you may not feel as passionately as you do about what you're trying to teach them. Stacy Swinea became a head coach at a very young age, and she brought to her first teams all of the fire and competitiveness that made her a great softball player. Swinea quickly learned that she could not expect of everyone else what she expected of herself. Instead, she had to maintain a balance between demanding commitment and giving young athletes space to grow and mature. In this piece, Stacy walks us through her own personal growth.

To see the impact that Stacy Swinea has had on the softball program at Davidson Academy, one needs only to look at the outfield scoreboard where the Lady Bears play: Just below the school logo, and above the area where the scores, innings, balls, strikes and outs are recorded, are the words "Stacy Swinea Field."

After more than 27 years of coaching, Swinea has tallied over 700 wins and three state titles. What's harder to see are the many ways that Coach Swinea has changed and matured over the years, as a coach.

"Coaching is tough," she says, noting that so much of what a good coach does falls into gray areas. At the beginning of Swinea's career, however, things seemed much more black-and-white.

All Softball, All the Time

Swinea got an early jump on her career as a head coach. She was 23 when she started coaching at Davidson Academy, and at 24, she became the head coach of the softball team.

At first, her thoughts were of winning seasons, championships and creating great softball players. For a while, that was enough. Swinea had players who were as driven as she was, and in that first season, it also helped that she had a team of "babies"—mostly eighth and ninth graders who hung on to every word their new coach said.

"Coaching was all I thought about," she says. "It was the most important thing in my life at the time."

It didn't take long for Swinea to begin seeing other things creeping into her neatly packaged world, though—namely, the countless hours spent handling the day-to-day issues that many of her girls were dealing with. The demands were various: giving girls a ride home when there was no one to pick them up from practice; helping to mend broken relationships; and just being there when the girls needed a shoulder to cry on.

A Changing Environment

Accepting that coaching meant teaching the game *and* being a surrogate parent was just one part of Swinea's growth. She also had to adapt to changes within the school itself.

When Swinea first arrived at Davidson Academy, she estimates that most of the students were from stable families. Today, that's not the case. Financial stress, difficulties at home and broken families are more common—and that means that Swinea has had to adapt how she works with the girls.

"People think, 'private school: money, money, money.' It's just not that way," says Swinea. The changing life situations means that Coach Swinea has to be more in tune with her girls' lives than ever before. "Coaching is a lot of me constantly learning," she says—and that often takes a number of turns.

Perhaps the most challenging issue is being more aware of the girls' home lives and situations. Softball is not an inexpensive sport: The equipment can get pricey, and the costs associated with traveling to far-off tournaments—a staple of competitive softball—can be high. On more than a few occasions, Swinea has had to dip into her own pockets to make sure that kids had the money to buy a meal. They don't come to her, asking for it; she just knows. It comes from paying attention to the little details in her players' lives.

The variety of backgrounds her players come from means that Swinea has to constantly adapt the ways that she reaches out to them. The old-school, authoritarian approach just won't work across the board. While some girls respond well to being yelled at, others can't take that kind of direct confrontation. Some girls need to be corrected immediately for their errors, while others learn better by stepping back and talking about things after the fact.

Swinea notes, "I'm always asking myself, How can I reach this kid?"

Baby and Me

Swinea credits motherhood for helping her to take some big steps forward as a coach. Among the most important lessons she's learned is just how busy her girls' lives really are.

"While they are dedicated and work very hard to be the best they can, they still have homework, families, social lives and the need to strengthen their own Christian lives," she says. "It wasn't until I had children of my own that I came to appreciate that kids need time to be kids."

One of the ways Swinea acknowledges this stress is by backing off at certain times. Usually, just before tournament time, she begins to see the signs of exhaustion—so she'll give the kids a break. They'll drop a practice and have a movie night, or they'll play a game of kickball. This flexibility gives them time to get away from softball and "reboot," as Swinea puts it.

Becoming a parent has also helped Swinea to appreciate the other side of the equation: the hurt that both the kids and their parents feel when they're on the bad end of a tough decision. "None of us wants to hurt a kid in any way. But sometimes, we do," she says.

Hurt can result because a coach has to bench a player for not performing; other times, a coach has to take action against someone because they've decided to shortcut the rules or do something detrimental to the team.

As a mom of two boys, Swinea has watched both of her sons be on the receiving end of difficult decisions. She's seen and felt the frustration that they go through, and it's made her think harder about how she treats her players.

"When making a decision about playing time for someone who has made bad choices, missed practices, bad attitudes, I always think, 'Would this be fair to the player on my team that is not very talented but is doing all the right things?'" Swinea says.

Sometimes, that means she makes decisions that cost her team games—and that's OK. "My girls see that I'm willing to step up and do what's right to teach a life lesson," she says.

An unexpected benefit of this approach has been improvement in her relationship with her player's parents, and Swinea says that she really doesn't have issues with her athletes' parents. "The parents see that I'm hard, but fair."

The Toughest Call

Every coach comes to those moments when they have to make a decision that sticks with them for the rest of their lives.

Swinea's moment came with an unlikely athlete—a girl who seemed to be living the high school dream. Popularity. A large group of friends. A good player. Smart. Kind-hearted. This girl was the kind of athlete that every coach wants on their team.

What many *didn't* see was the girl's eating disorder.

Swinea poured enormous amounts of time into this athlete. She talked with her, talked with her mother, and even rode in the ambulance with the girl when her cramping from lack of food became so severe that she couldn't stand.

Everything came to a head as the team was preparing to leave for a tournament in Gulf Shores, Alabama.

"We were fixing to leave, and I just realized, I can't take this girl with us," recalls Swinea. "The toughest decision was to call her mom and to tell her, 'I can't take her. She needs to be here with you, and you two need to figure some things out.'"

Swinea had no way of knowing what would happen. It could have turned the girl around, or it could have brought her world down and sent her spinning out of control. As it turns out, the girl recovered, returned the next year, and helped the team win a state championship.

There just comes a point where, notes Swinea, "You've got to be able to do what you're supposed to do."

A Complete Coach

Don't mistake growth for softening, though. Swinea is still a demanding coach. As her girls know, "You don't mess with coach Swinea."

Unlike earlier in her career, Swinea is now a complete coach. She sees the whole picture. Perhaps most importantly, she has come to appreciate that sometimes, things just don't mean as much to her athletes as they do to her.

Swinea's completeness shines most brightly at the end of each season, at the team banquet. At these events, it's not uncommon for coaches to call up each of the seniors and say something about them. Swinea makes sure that she talks about every girl in the program. It's a job that "takes hours of preparation," she says, but is one that she does because she wants each athlete to feel important. It's the one time each year when her girls' parents get to really see what a complete coach looks like.

Recently, a parent wasn't planning to attend the banquet because her daughter hadn't been able to play. Swinea encouraged her to come anyway. This parent did, and as Swinea recalls, "she was in tears at the end." The mom had no idea how important her daughter was to the team, to Coach Swinea, and to her teammates.

"I've had a lot of good teams, and a lot of special relationships with girls over the years," Swinea says. "It's fun seeing all them now, as they're having families. Those are the rewards of coaching. When they come back."

A lifetime of development as a coach isn't captured in the sign along the outfield fence at Davidson Academy; it's captured in the heart of every kid that Swinea has helped develop over her career.

17

Al Fracassa, from Dave Yeager

"He doesn't take credit for anything."

—Dave Yeager

Football

Head coach: Royal Oak Shrine High School (1960–1968), Brother Rice High School (1969–2013)

Perhaps no coach in this book has gone through more changes during his career than Al Fracassa. In this chapter, Dave Yeager—who played for Fracassa at Royal Oak Shrine High School in the early 1960s—recounts how Fracassa adapted to players from the 1960s to the 2010s.

On Friday evenings in the fall, Dave Yeager navigates his car down a tree-lined street in Warren, Michigan, to a modest home. There, he picks up a friend he first met in 1964—at Royal Oak Shrine High School—and drives him to the game at nearby Brother Rice High School.

When this gentleman and Yeager first met, "friend" wasn't yet the word Yeager used to describe him; "coach" was the word. Coach Al Fracassa.

Yeager played for Fracassa at Royal Oak Shrine High School, when Coach Fracassa was just getting started. In two words, Yeager summarizes the approach taken by the then-young coach: "Organization, discipline."

In the 1960s, organization and discipline were accompanied by a lot of yelling. Yeager still recalls his freshman season, when underdog Shrine tied powerhouse Notre Dame 0-0 in the Soup Bowl, the game played to determine the Catholic League champion. The winner moved on to play the public school champion. To decide who would advance, the league looked to whomever had gained the most yards in the game. As it turned out, Notre Dame had four more and, as a result, advanced.

Since no one expected that Shrine stood a chance against Notre Dame, many coaches would have chalked up the season to a great year. Not Fracassa. "The next year," Yeagar says, Fracassa "became very, very intense. That motivated us. Kids at that time could take that kind of hollering and criticism. If you did well, he would still criticize you."

To many of us today, such an approach would be looked down upon. For Yeager, to focus on the yelling is to miss the point.

A Deeper Connection

Spend some time with Yeagar and Fracassa on a Friday night at the game and it becomes apparent that there was a lot more to the relationship between coach and player than hard-nosed intimidation.

Former players from 10, 20 or 30 years ago come up to Fracassa, Yeager says, and "he remembers every one of them. He spends five or 10 minutes talking to them." Most astonishing is the depth of the conversations, Yeager notes, as Fracassa seems to know every detail of their lives.

Former players tell Fracassa how he changed their lives: how his lessons stayed with them in their family life, their work life, their social lives. The depth of this impact was most notably on display at a banquet convened for Coach Fracassa's retirement, where 700 former players showed up. The stories of love and respect are too numerous to recount here, but one, in particular, sticks out in Yeager's mind.

"There was a kid at Brother Rice when Coach first started who had some discipline problems. Troubles with family, school. Coach sat down and wrote out a list of things that he needed to do to turn it around," he recalls. "This kid had this piece of paper in his wallet—he'd had it for 45 years. Coach Fracassa read it onstage."

Fracassa's concern didn't stop with his players, either. Athlete or non-athlete, boy or girl, able or disabled, there was no end to the lengths he would go to give of himself. Early in his teaching and coaching years, every student was required to run 1 mile in order to successfully complete gym class. Yeagar recalls a legally blind student struggling to fulfill the requirement. "Fracassa ran every step of that mile with him," Yeager says, "encouraging him with each step he took."

The bottom line, according to Yeager, is that everything Fracassa does is for everyone else. "He takes no credit for anything."

An Innate Ability to Change

That his players are his first concern has been evident to those who've watched Coach Fracassa evolve over the years.

Fracassa has kept what's worked—the aphorisms; the willingness to learn all the little details about the people who play for him (and remember them); writing letters annually to each of his senior players—and has adjusted it to today's players' temperaments and abilities.

Yeager admits that today's players could not—probably would not—tolerate the kind of practices that Fracassa put him through in the 1960s. And yet Fracassa continued to win through the '70s, '80s, '90s, '00s and even '10s. "His last three years at Brother Rice," Yeager notes, "Fracassa won three state titles in a row."

Fracassa may have had good players, but if those players were not pulling in the same direction, the team could not have won. In his latter years, Coach Fracassa continued to get his players to pull in the same direction—even without the yelling.

"I think kids are looking for guidance no matter what time period you're from," Yeager says." You just have to present it properly so that they can accept it. [Fracassa] had the same impact on those last three teams that he had on me."

A Rare Gem

Yeager's appreciation for Coach Fracassa only grew in the years after high school. A gifted athlete in his own right, Yeager played baseball at Eastern Michigan University and then returned to work with Coach Fracassa at Brother Rice, where he coached the freshman team for two years and then spent one year with the varsity team. (One of his players was Kevin Hart, profiled in Chapter 30.)

Yeager then jumped to coaching at the college level, earning a slot as a graduate assistant at his alma mater. It was a life-changing move.

"These college coaches were all in it for themselves. I got really turned off by it," he says. "Got my master's in accounting and became a CPA."

Yeager's career took off when he applied the lessons from his high school playing days to his work, first with pizza chain Little Caesars and then with another pizza chain, Hungry Howie's.

What is the lesson that proved most useful to him in business?

"Everyone makes mistakes, and the team has to pick you up and cover for those mistakes," Yeager says. "It's great for business, because you need everyone focused on the same goal."

Throughout his life, Yeager has tried to carry all of Coach Fracassa's lessons with him. By his own admission, though, "it's tough."

Perhaps there's no better example of how Yeager has embraced Coach Fracassa's lessons than the drives that Yeager makes to Fracassa's house on those Fridays. Yeager does it not for himself, but as a gift to everyone who knew the coach—and to those who are, for the first time, being introduced to the man who still lives to do for others.

Part IV:
Coaches and Their Communities

"When the good guys stop letting you play with them,
the bad guys have a field day."
—Shone Evans

18

Michael Groves

*"I coach from my heart, with the goal of having
every player have a positive experience."*

Baseball

Head coach: Monterey High School (1980–present)

*There's an adage that if you can change just one life, you've been success-
ful. Coaches have the opportunity to touch many lives, as the players they
work with usually change annually. Yet few coaches have the type of impact
that changes not only the lives of their players, but their communities as well.
Michael Groves is one such coach. His success as a baseball coach speaks for
itself: The list of players' lives that he's affected, for the better, is long. But it's
the impact on the town of Monterey, California, that truly sets apart Groves'
life from that of most coaches. It's a trajectory that no coach can hope to
recreate, but the tools and imagination that Groves employs are available to
each of us.*

During the summers when he was home from college in 1979 and
1980, Michael Groves was coaching summer league baseball and umpir-
ing junior college baseball games in his native Monterey, California. A
more-senior umpire, James Lancaster, saw something in Groves and told
him, "You need to be a coach. You call someone out, but then you want to
explain about their footwork."

Groves didn't think much of it, but Lancaster did. When the head
coaching position at Monterey High School became available in 1980,

Lancaster approached the school principal and asked him to hire Groves. The principal did so. Groves agreed to the job, but could only promise one year: He was starting a business at the time, and couldn't imagine having the availability necessary.

Forty years later, Groves is still coaching. The players call him "Grover," and they call their beloved game of baseball "Groverball." How he achieved his success—19 league championships, 33 Central Coast Section playoff appearances, 3 Section championships, a win-loss percentage of 67%, and induction into the California State Baseball Coaches Hall of Fame—is easily summed up. As Groves succinctly states, "You create a space for young people to have a way to improve their craft."

One can't simply copy the outward expressions of how Groves achieves success; after all, the way that he creates space for young people is deeply enmeshed with the intense work he has done to become a better and more inclusive leader. His success is also anchored in two relationships: the one he shares with Monterey Peninsula College, and the one he has with his wife of 28 years, Laurie, who does with student-artists/dancers what he does with student-athletes.

Laurie summed up both his and her success in a simple equation: "You create a climate that is all-accepting, that's inclusive, and safe, and you watch things flourish. You love them unconditionally and learn right along with them. That's the joy where Michael and I connected."

Becoming a Better Version of Yourself

Groves' passion for baseball—and ability to coach—has never been in doubt. Groves grew up around the game, and his father was the head of the local Little League organization. Groves' father also created the fields in Carmel Valley in 1966, which became a place for his 12-year-old son to hone his pitching skills.

Groves went on to pitch for Carmel High School and did well enough to play at Monterey Peninsula College under legendary Coach Chris Pappas. It was the important lessons around inclusion that Pappas taught Groves—as much as the finer points of baseball—that would set him on the path to a concept currently known as "transformative coaching."

In transformative coaching, a coach is not just teaching the game; he is developing kids' social and emotional IQs and skills, too. "Pappas did a lot of work with Special Olympics," Groves recalls, "which inspired me to be more inclusive."

Groves has spent his entire life working at becoming more inclusive. He points to the work he did with men's groups and with the National Coalition Building Institute, which helps leaders understand the systemic working behind the "-isms": racism, sexism, classism and ageism. The latter has become particularly important to Groves' work. "Youth, like everyone else," he says, "want to be treated with the same respect as one would give adults."

Another individual who has shaped Groves' growth is legendary UCLA basketball coach John Wooden, with his "Pyramid of Success." Wooden's Pyramid of Success stresses the importance of building a team foundation that will survive even when outward occurrences are not to one's liking—which almost always happens at some point in a game as difficult as baseball.

The Positive Coaching Alliance is another organization that Groves has learned from and whose concepts his Monterey High School players are aware of. This organization's focus is to first be aware, and then to transform into positive expressions the negative verbal and physical communications that we are often unaware of. Groves preaches this last concept relentlessly.

"We have a goal every day," says Groves, "to make ourselves better, make our teammates better, and make the game better." Then, Groves continues, "there are those 'out of the box' things I come up to when I trust my intuition. Laurie is always bringing some kind of breathing, mind-body therapy, visualization, injury prevention techniques to the party.... It's fun."

Then there is the leadership model that Groves brings from his successful environmental consulting firm. Rather than appointing one or two captains, as most teams do, Groves has created a leadership group of five to seven players, selected by returning leadership members and the coach. This group meets for a luncheon before the season begins, and together they set goals, objectives, communication protocols and leaders' responsibilities.

The role model that Groves is—and the lessons he imparts—are not lost on his players, either. One of Groves' player-leaders is Michael Mugan, who speaks for the whole team when he says, "We knew he had a lot of responsibilities. He was the president of a successful business, he showed up to practice in a suit and tie before he changed [into his uniform], and sometimes he'd be in his car on a phone call in the parking lot when we arrived. But he was always there: He never missed one game or one practice, ever."

Gratitude and Traditions

From his work to improve himself, Groves also developed a deep appreciation for the power of gratitude.

"The point of gratitude," he says, is that it positively shapes how you "reflect on your day and your life." On a basic level, gratitude is as simple as "waking up every day and having three gratitudes you say to yourself," says Groves.

His wife, Laurie, has also been critical in helping him to embrace gratitude.

Laurie is a dance educator who directed the Monterey Bay Dance Company, an organization comprised of students from three high schools within the Monterey Peninsula Unified School District and Monterey Peninsula College. The company has a 50-year history as a multicultural performing dance company and includes students of all ethnicities, races, colors, creeds, religions, sizes and abilities.

Both Laurie and Michael recall one student, in particular, who was challenged with weight issues. Laurie remembers some people laughing at her under their breath when she came out to dance a Mahalia Jackson modern/ballet solo piece. Those who had laughed were moved to tears soon after she started, stunned by her beauty, grace and technical skill.

Laurie recounts some women rushing backstage, saying that this student's performance had given them the permission to dance—no matter what size they were.

That experience highlights the power of gratitude: to learn to appreciate beauty and inspiration wherever it's found. Gratitude is best experienced in community, too.

To amplify gratitude, Groves has successfully wedded tradition to moments of profound gratitude. Groves has been key in establishing many such moments, but perhaps the most important and touching is the one that occurs at every home game—when the team walks past the stands to the bronze statue bust of Frank Sollecito Jr., No. 16.

Frank Sollecito Jr., or "Frankie," was a star pitcher and scholar at MHS who had earned a full scholarship to play baseball at the University of California, Berkeley. His life was cut short, though—by leukemia. He was diagnosed his senior year of high school, and although he never had the opportunity to don the blue and gold of UC Berkeley, a spontaneous act by Groves ensured that Frankie had one last chance to wear his high school jersey. That moment is burned in the community's memory.

Frankie had missed most of his senior season. Weakened by chemotherapy, he had done well just to get out of the hospital and sit on the bench for MHS' Central Coast Section, a playoff game held at San Jose Municipal Stadium. The thought of playing was out of the question.

Groves could see that Frankie desperately wanted to get in, though. Late in the game, he told Frankie to warm up. "But coach," the young man demurred, "I don't have a jersey."

Instinctively, Groves took off his own jersey and handed it to Frankie, sending him in to pitch. Frankie had lost considerable velocity on his pitches, but he managed to force two quick outs with a ground ball and an infield pop-up, then struck out the last batter. Fans on both sides (who were well aware of Frankie's diagnosis and struggles) erupted. There wasn't a dry eye in the house, and no concern was paid to the final score.

Today, as players make their way to Frankie's statue before every home game, they give thanks. They also honor his memory and embrace what has become Groves' mantra: "Be present. Have fun. And above all … play ball!" This expression captures the gratitude we should all feel just for being alive and able-bodied. It also captures the spirit of MHS baseball.

Monterey Peninsula College

Groves' passion for baseball, his embracing gratitude and his commitment to inclusion have also found a home at Monterey Peninsula College. Until very recently, Lyndon Schutzler—Groves' best friend from their shared early years in baseball—was the school's athletic director. Together, Schutzler and Groves have raised millions of dollars for both the college and high school athletes in the community of Monterey.

Groves actively encourages many of his players to continue their playing careers at Monterey Peninsula College. The current MPC coach, Danny Phillips, also happens to be a Monterey High School alumnus who played for Groves.

Both Michael and Laurie have been tireless advocates for their student athletes and student dancers/artists, encouraging them to enroll at MPC as a first step to their higher education. MPC has been a friend to them, too.

When Seaside High School and Monterey High School made cuts to their art programs—including dance programs—Laurie turned to Schutzler. Laurie hoped to create a college outreach dance program that would ensure that students within the district would not go without quality dance education, and that the Monterey Bay Dance Company—funded by the Monterey County Cultural Council—would remain active.

MPC provided a stage for the kids to work on.

"And," Laurie notes, "for the kids to be in my program, they had to enroll at MPC, which really started their college careers. I had kids that never dreamed of going to college."

Always Rooting for the Underdog

As Laurie succinctly states, "We are always rooting for the underdog." It is this, perhaps more than anything, that best explains why Coach Groves' focus is on inclusivity and community in everything he does—from his personal life, to business, to the field.

He is as competitive as anyone when it comes to what goes on between the lines during a game, and he is constantly looking for opportunities to include his players in situations so that they will achieve success. Success, however, has many facets.

"I wanted to create a culture where the community is involved," Groves says. "I coach from my heart, with the goal of having every player have a positive experience."

None of this would have been possible, though, if they hadn't continued to do their own emotional and spiritual work, notes Laurie. "Those students are our lives, our stories," she says.

When talking about her husband, Laurie adds, "He is like a big oak tree. Michael plants his roots—and he stays."

And *that* is how one creates a consistent culture in which everyone can grow.

19

Heang Uy

"We take everybody."

Wrestling

Head coach: North Henderson High School (2000–present)

Sports is known for helping to break barriers. In Hendersonville, North Carolina, Coach Heang Uy is tearing down barriers with his wrestling program: barriers of distrust that exist between locals and immigrants. Uy is an immigrant, as are many of the students who are involved in his wrestling program at North Henderson High School. Over 20 years, Uy has done more than build a winning culture: He's built a team that everyone in the community—Black, White, Hispanic and East Asian—can rally around.

In the years following the Vietnam War, a sizeable number of Cambodian, Laotian and Vietnamese refugees were resettled in the United States. One of those refugees was a very young Heang Uy, whose parents braved the journey to bring him to America.

They settled in the western part of North Carolina in the small community of Hendersonville. There, Uy grew up and attended West Henderson High School. He excelled both academically and on the wrestling team. When he left for college, he thought he'd begun his journey away from his adopted hometown. After graduating from Elon University with a degree in History, however, a job opened back home at North Henderson High

School. "I took the job thinking I'd teach for a few years and move on to something else," Uy recalls. "Twenty years later, here I am."

In his time at North, Uy has continued the tradition of excellence in wrestling that his predecessor established. That's impressive enough. What is most interesting is that a considerable number of the athletes who flock to Uy's program often come from the roughly one-third of the student body that is Hispanic. These are kids who, before coming to the United States, were most likely not even aware of the sport. Wrestling is, after all, relatively unknown in Mexico and Central America.

A Common Experience

The Hispanic students at North share with Uy a powerful experience: that of being the immigrant. "The whole migrant process and why people move is something that is very personal to me," Uy says.

Many of the Hispanic students at North arrive to the area with their families, set to work the agricultural fields in and around the city. In addition to having to adjust to a new culture and a new language, these students also face a country that, as of late, has not proven welcoming to outsiders.

"There is certainly fear in our community," says Uy. "We have some students whose legal status is fine, but they worry about their parents." Uy understands the instability in his students' lives, and he goes more than the extra mile to help them adjust. "We've had to meet them halfway, accommodate them, and help them," Uy says.

When kids have to miss practice because they have to drive their parents somewhere—parents who can't get their own driver's license—Uy understands. "They know that we are going to support them and advocate for them," he says. "We've used our position to fight and advocate for our community."

Bridging with Wrestling

The sport of wrestling also connects coach and athlete. When Uy got to middle school, he wanted to play basketball. When that didn't work out, the wrestling coach asked him to join his team. Uy did, and he thrived in the sport during his middle school and high school years. From seventh grade through 12th grade, Uy went from knowing next to nothing about wrestling to becoming a critical member of a team that won the state wrestling championship his senior year.

"Wrestling is a great sport for people on their way," says Uy. "It's not a sport you have to do your whole life to be good at."

If your experience with wrestling is limited to what you see on television, Uy believes that you haven't seen the beauty and power of the sport. Wrestling is a physical chess match: It requires mastering a series of moves and countermoves to outsmart and outmaneuver the opponent. In addition, unlike the skills needed to play baseball and basketball and football, one can learn and master wrestling's basic skills fairly quickly.

Uy's commitment to the immigrant population and his passion for wrestling has endeared both him and his program to the teachers and administrators at North.

"We take everybody," said Uy. "We take ragamuffins. Teachers and counselors send kids our way because they feel the structure will be good for them. We take the castaways and hold them to high expectations."

Family

For kids who have to constantly worry that their families will be ripped apart without warning, the wrestling family that Uy has built provides an island of stability and security.

"It all comes down to family," says Coach Uy. "We're going to defend each other. Fight for each other. The family needs to be supported, and we all need to take care of each other." Family members also push one another, and Uy is strict about holding his wrestlers accountable—to him, to themselves, and to their teammates.

One example of that accountability was on display at a recent state tournament. A wrestler who was favored to be a finalist and possibly win a state title was unexpectedly disqualified during skin check. (Skin checks occur before every tournament. Athletes are examined to ensure that they have no rashes or infections showing that might be transmitted to an opponent.)

"It was so horrible for that kid," Uy recalls. "He was a senior. He could have gone home and sulked, but he stayed the entire weekend and supported his teammates."

The occurrence was also a horrible blow for the team. Although the team finished second in the state that year, had their teammate wrestled and won a few matches, North could have won the state title that, so far, has eluded Uy's program.

The loss certainly hurt, but Uy takes a lot of pride in the resiliency and commitment that his wrestlers displayed. It's the same resiliency he sees year in and year out. This is a family that stays together.

The community, too, is rallying around this team. When the team does well or a North wrestler wins a state title, it's a cause for celebration across the entire Hendersonville community. "We're something positive," Uy says.

That's quite an achievement for a coach who originally thought he'd move on from education, toward another career and other opportunities. As it turns out, he fits best in Hendersonville.

"I'm just really proud of our wrestling program," says Uy. "It's going to be one of the legacies of my life."

20

Neil Duffy

"Every moment matters."

Boys' lacrosse, girls' basketball

Coach: Norfolk Academy

During the summer I witnessed a remarkable event. Members of the girls' basketball program at Norfolk Academy publicly thanking individuals for helping make them who they are, and honoring them by dedicating a game to them.

It's a tradition begun by Neil Duffy, who has spent a lifetime thinking about and working to teach the simple act of gratitude. Duffy isn't shy about expressing his gratitude to those who've made his life possible—people like his high school lacrosse coach, Don Holmes.

In this story, we get to see how a simple act has led to an experience that Duffy's athletes carry with them across the country as they leave Norfolk Academy. A simple act spurred by a lifetime of gratefulness, and the remarkable expression of gratitude a former student and athlete, serving in the U.S. Special Forces, showed his teacher.

When it comes to building programs, Neil Duffy is all about the small things.

As a lacrosse and basketball coach, and former lacrosse athlete at the United States Naval Academy, Duffy is much more at home trying to inspire his athletes by picking up a stick and getting in the mix to demonstrate foot work and body position than he is delivering impassioned speeches and spending countless hours on Xs and Os.

These latter tactics are all driven by "motivation" he says. And motivation "is all about telling kids what they have to do: run harder, work harder." It's a tough sell, he acknowledges. Instead, Duffy has learned from many coaches over the years the difference between motivation and what he calls "inspiration," which by contrast he says, "is ... about helping them to be their best, and letting them do the work."

Duffy has been both coaches in his career. "I was a motivator longer than I wanted to be," he says. "I'm sure I made my fair share of mistakes, and I broke more than a few clipboards" along the way. Grand speeches and acts of motivation have their place, but it's the small acts of inspiration, Duffy has found, that lead to something far richer.

At the heart of inspiration for Duffy is the simple act of gratitude.

It Starts with Serving Others

In important ways, gratitude has always played a central role in Duffy's life. It has shaped him from his earliest days as a child in New York, to his time as a student and lacrosse player at the United States Naval Academy, to his more than 30 years of coaching boys' lacrosse and girls' basketball at the high school level.

His parents grounded him in that ideal. "They were very community minded," he says. "Their faith was very important to them. Serving others mattered to them. They grew up in the Great Depression and WWII, and my mother was very clear in expressing to us that she didn't need birthday or Christmas gifts because she had what she needed."

The importance of gratitude grew for Duffy during his years at the Naval Academy and as an active-duty officer. In particular, he admired the leaders who did everything within their power to care for their sailors. Their efforts, he says, were "inspiring."

Duffy carried that commitment to serving others into the classroom after he left the Navy. He began at Nansemond-Suffolk Academy in Virginia, then left for Norfolk Academy, where he is now in his 28th year.

The lessons in gratitude Duffy took from his parents, fellow officers, coaches, and teammates were with him from the beginning of his coaching career. He just wasn't intentional in teaching it. He lived it, and his players picked up on it. Early on, that this was true was evidenced in the relationships he built, and the willingness of his players to thank him by staying in touch and sharing their information with him.

"Some of my [early] players were successful enough to play in college," he says. "I would watch them play and learn a lot, and I'd also ask them questions. 'What do your coaches talk about?'"

His players were more than happy to share that information with him—something they surely wouldn't have done had they not respected and admired their high school coach.

Duffy calls this information "cyclic feedback" and finds it extremely valuable in his coaching. "I get to take [that information] right back to the people that I am coaching right now." It was this commitment to his players and ongoing relationships with them that was a key to his winning the 2019 USA Lacrosse's Gerald J. Carrol Jr. Exemplary Coaching Award.

As time moved on, Duffy began thinking a bit deeper about gratitude and its role in his career and the lives of his students.

"I've heard coaches say, 'Things start to change when you go to their weddings,'" he says. "Then you begin to see what it means in their lives." He began to appreciate how much "every moment matters" to the people in his charge. "If you're too sarcastic to them. Or if you're late to practice. Or you're not attentive enough to language. Your players will notice that."

It was a selfless moment in 2008, however, that moved Duffy to really think about gratitude and the role it played in his coaching life. As important, how much he wanted to be intentional about teaching that trait to the players he worked with daily.

This Is Backwards

When asked to name the players who've meant the most to him in his career, Duffy demurs. "There's been so many," he said. "I'm not sure I want to order them. It's kind of like trying to name your favorite children."

Nonetheless, there are moments with certain individuals that stick out.

One of those individuals is a player who chose a career in the military. He spent much of his time with U.S. Special Forces—the elite who carry out the most dangerous missions our nation executes—the vast majority of which people never know about.

Returning home after one such mission, this individual went into Duffy's class and presented him with a full-size American flag and an accompanying certificate. And not just any flag.

Duffy says that "He was doing an operation to take care of what they needed to do. He carried on his person and stuffed into his gear a full-size U.S. flag." A flag that was on or with him throughout this particular mission.

"I was completely blown away," Duffy said, "and I asked why he would do something like that."

The soldier answered him with one word: "gratitude."

As Duffy got over the shock, he thought, "This is backwards, I should be thanking you."

Weeks passed, and Duffy found in this moment an opportunity to intentionally help his players understand, and express, gratitude.

With the permission of the Special Ops soldier, Duffy created the Play to Honor program. A simple, one-day event that's meant to replicate in a small way what Duffy experienced that day in his classroom.

He used it for the first time with his girl's basketball team. He asked his players to dedicate a game to someone—just as the Special Ops soldier had done for him. "They invited a guest to a game, and dedicated the game to them. We also wanted them to publicly thank these people."

The response from the people on the receiving end of the gesture, Duffy says, has been as powerful for them as it was for him when the soldier gave him that flag. "A single kind act from a single kind person has trickled out over several hundred folks now."

Duffy hopes that others will follow this lead. He notes that the program is not copyrighted, and that anyone who wants to can use that model. And the Special Forces soldier who started it all? He's grateful that people are benefiting from it, and supports anyone who wants to use it.

A Larger Community

What began at Nansemond-Suffolk Academy and is now happening at Norfolk Academy is creating a community that extends far beyond the campuses' walls in Virginia. It's happening because one man has been taught by his students and has now lived, and found ways to teach, gratitude.

It's a lesson that Neil Duffy's parents, his siblings, his Naval Academy classmates and naval officers all modeled for him. Now, in a world obsessed with social media and self-promotion, Duffy is teaching others to take some time, and thank someone publicly for helping them on their journey toward success.

Duffy hopes that his students will take that lesson into the world with them and share it with others.

The Gerald J. Carroll, Jr. Exemplary Coaching Award, established in memory of Gerry Carroll, is given annually to one boys' high school coach nationwide who reflects the attributes of the award's namesake. Coach Carroll spent a good part of his brief 46 years playing, watching, and coaching lacrosse. Greater than his love for the sport, however, was his commitment to give back to young people some of the lifetime of lessons he himself took from the game.

Nominees for the Carroll Award, established in 1994, must demonstrate support and care for players in their growth and development as young adults and leaders on and off the playing field. Nominees must also be members in good standing of USA Lacrosse. The recipient is chosen by a committee comprised of Carroll friends and family.

21

Fouad Zaban

"It's my duty to live my life a certain way."

Football

Head coach: Fordson High School (2007–present)

There's much about Fordson High School that screams "middle America": It was built in 1928 and named for the son of business tycoon Henry Ford; its mascot, the Tractors, derives from the machines that Ford Motor Company was building at the time; and to top it off, the school is crazy about high school football.

Were Henry Ford alive today, he'd likely still recognize the facilities and passion for sports, but he would not recognize the student body. Situated in Dearborn, Michigan—home to one of the largest Muslim communities in the Western Hemisphere—today's Fordson is more in line with the "American dream" than with Americana.

Fouad Zaban grew up in Dearborn, played football at Fordson, and has been the school's head coach since 2007. He understands well the prejudice and outright scorn that his players face when they walk out of the confines of Dearborn. But for the four years he has them, Zaban uses football to teach his guys how to deal with a world that may well not like you simply because of your name.

To teach his players, he's put a simple, two-word motto at the center of the Fordson football program: no excuses.

"We adopted this expression precisely as a way to deal with bigotry and racism," says Zaban.

The way Zaban delivers his message certainly stands out, too. Whereas many use this type of expression to simply mean, "Don't make excuses—just do it" (a la Nike), Zaban's approach appears to be more nuanced. His approach blends family with discipline and determination.

Family: the Cornerstone

Zaban is committed to his faith, and at the core of Islam is family—a concept that includes respect for all family members. This is the cornerstone of "no excuses" for Zaban.

"Kids are kids," he says, and just because the vast majority of Zaban's players are Muslim, that doesn't mean they don't struggle with the same issues that every teenager struggles with—including parental rebellion. Zaban is adamant that his players learn to respect their parents, "even when the parent is wrong," he says.

Everyone who has ever coached has had to deal with less-than-ideal parents—and, on the flip side, with players who don't show their parents an appropriate level of respect. One parent-player dynamic continues to stick in Zaban's memory.

This player's dad "wasn't a good father figure," Zaban recalls. He wasn't abusive (which is a different, more serious, issue), he just was "not good to Mom and kids. My thing to my player was, 'Hey, he's still your dad. You still have to show him respect. … Don't get in confrontations. Support your mom and siblings.'"

Rather than dealing with the issues he faced in his life, the young man wanted only to let out his frustrations on his dad. That, Zaban knows, is ultimately destructive for everyone.

Once you learn to respect those closest to you, it becomes easier to take the next step in living a no-excuses lifestyle.

Discipline: Growing Into Responsibility

There are certain things that a player can control: his effort, his work ethic, and the execution of his assignment. There are far more things that a player can't control, though. To develop as an individual and as a team, players must learn to handle the ups and downs caused by forces beyond their control. This requires discipline and a singular focus on one's task.

In the case of football, it's the officials who often will test a player's discipline. A great example of this was captured in a documentary on the Fordson football program, entitled, *Fordson: Faith, Fasting, and Football.* (Available on YouTube at https://www.youtube.com/watch?v=l45Ekl_5uuQ)

In the first half of the annual clash with cross-town rival Dearborn High School, Fordson saw its all-everything wide receiver ejected for getting two personal fouls on the same play. The team also had a touchdown called back for another foul, as well as a series of flags for late hits and various illegal actions.

In the locker room, Zaban took his players to task for their lack of discipline. On the officials and their calls, he said, "How many times have we told you to keep your mouths shut? You know it's going to be called on us. We told you that."

But at the moment he could have blamed the officials, Zaban turned it around. "You gave these officials the right to throw every little flag possible. I don't blame them. I truly don't. … I blame us. You've given them the right to do everything they've done out there."

Determination: Moving Beyond the Obstructions

If you can respect your family and learn to be disciplined in the face of countervailing winds, then you can exercise determination. It's this concept that not only matters on the field, but allows individuals to battle racism and bigotry throughout life. It may well be fair to say that Zaban doesn't talk about determination so much as he lives it.

"It's my duty to live my life a certain way. … Not to give people fuel for fire," he says. "Not to give them any weapons for them to use against us."

After four years with Zaban, players have countless times seen him live out his determination to do what is right. It's something Zaban never tires of doing. If there is one frustration, it's only that he can't reach everyone.

"I know that we're teaching the right lessons, but I … (also) know that my heart gets broken a lot, from when kids make mistakes," he says. "I know that they're kids, and I keep giving them chances."

In Zaban's mind, there is no excuse for doing less.

22

Fouad Zaban, from Ibrahim 'Abe' Ahmad

"We knew him as Haj Zaban, growing up."
—**Ibrahim "Abe" Ahmad**

Football

Head coach: Fordson High School (2007–present)

In a nation as mobile as America, where children often look forward to traveling far from home for college or work (with their parents' blessings), it's easy to forget that there are communities where leaving is neither encouraged nor viewed as something to be excited about. Some people have legitimate fears about what can happen outside the safety of the community they were born into and raised in. In this chapter, Abe Ahmad talks about his experience being raised in "the bubble" of Dearborn, Michigan, and how his coach helped him embrace the challenge of moving outside the bubble.

Ibrahim "Abe" Ahmad is like a lot of other young, smart, idealistic people. He holds strong political views; he is passionate about public service and working in government; and he sometimes goes door-to-door, trying to convince people to vote for the candidates he believes in. He wants to make a difference in the world.

However, Ahmad is unlike many of the people he grew up with in Dearborn, Michigan, in one important way: He isn't afraid to travel outside "the bubble."

"The bubble"—that's the term that Ibrahim and others use to describe East Dearborn. In a nation that has seen anti-Muslim sentiment rising,

East Dearborn is a safe haven. Resident parents often worry that children who travel beyond the community's confines will face discrimination—or worse—simply because of their name.

"The kids grow up here, and [they] end up living here and working here and raising their kids here," says Ahmad. "Most people in this community appreciate the high concentration of people of the same race, ethnicity and religion as them, and thus, would much rather stay and live amongst those that are more like they are."

One of the reasons they stay—beyond safety—is the strong connections that people there build with family, their faith community and their high school, Fordson.

And the person that many look up to at Fordson is the head football coach, Fouad Zaban.

Haj

Ahmad played for Zaban at Fordson, but he knew of him long before he became interested in football.

"We knew him as *Haj* Zaban growing up," says Ahmad. (*Haj* is a term of high honor given to a trusted community figure who has made the pilgrimage to Mecca.) To Ahmad, Zaban was nothing short of a pillar in his community and a father figure.

The first time Ahmad encountered Zaban as someone other than a respected elder was when he started playing youth football. Though the Dearborn Youth Football Program isn't connected to the local high schools, the coaches take a great interest in the youth program.

By the time that Ahmad made his way to Fordson, he had come to appreciate Zaban for more than the position he held in the community. Zaban was the person who taught Ahmad that the only way to battle the systemic racism he and others faced was to rise above the storm and embrace the enemy as a brother.

"Arab Americans and Muslim Americans deal with a lot of racism," says Ahmad. Recalling a playoff game at Monroe, a town south of Dearborn and about halfway between Detroit and Toledo, he recalls, "As we were leaving the stadium, we heard chants of 'camels' and 'terrorists.'"

Striking back never entered his mind because of what Zaban stresses to his players. As Ahmad recalls, Zaban teaches that, "If you give into ignorance and hate, you are giving them importance that they don't deserve. Especially people who don't respect us."

Outside the Bubble

When faced with such prejudice, Zaban teaches his players to not give in to it, but to ignore it.

"If we react with anger and frustration to racism and unfair treatment from the opposing team, fans or even the refs," says Ahmad, "it's not only going to reflect badly on us, but on the community as a whole." It isn't fair, but it's reality. And Zaban is nothing if not about teaching his players to face reality.

Ahmad proudly recalls what Zaban would say about every team Fordson played: "I don't care who they are—Black, white, whatever—when the game is over, you'd better go over there and hug them and shake their hands. They're your brothers." That has been the lesson that has most stuck with Ahmad, giving him the strength to venture outside the community.

Ahmad is no stranger to appreciation for the country at large, either.

"My father came from Lebanon," he says, noting that his mother's parents did, too. They, like many of the other families in Dearborn, "come from places where you simply don't have the opportunities you have here in America, the greatest nation on earth," says Ahmad. "We understand what this country offers better than many people do," he adds, because the memories of being in lands where opportunities *aren't* available is never more than a conversation away.

Ahmad knows who he is. He knows what it is to be a person of honor. He knows what it takes to stand up and face adversity. He owes this to his coach, his family, and his Dearborn community—and he is carrying that message beyond the streets of Dearborn, to those who will listen.

Outside the bubble may be uncomfortable, but Ahmad isn't afraid. He has a *Haj* leading the way.

23

Shone Evans

*"When the good guys stop letting you play with
them, the bad guys have a field day."*

Football

Head coach: La Marque High School (2018–present)

La Marque High School sits just 15 miles from the vacation city of Galveston, Texas. Life in La Marque is no holiday, though.

Like much of southern Texas, the city has been hit by a wave of hurricanes—most recently Hurricane Harvey, in 2017. Whereas the nearby communities of Galveston and Houston were able to bounce back, La Marque was not. Natural disasters aren't the community's only setbacks, though. Further complicating matters was the Texas Education Agency's annexation of the school district in 2016. The community takes pride in its high school, but persistent academic problems and mismanagement of funds forced the state to take over, dissolve the district and annex it to a neighboring school district, Texas City ISD.

The town is trying to regain its identity, and it's looking to Shone Evans to be a big part of finding its way back. In 2018, Evans was named head football coach at the school that has known five state titles and 10 title game appearances. It's been 10 years since the Cougars have played in a state championship game, and for most of those years, the team—like the community—has been struggling to get back to where it once was.

Evans brings two qualities to the job that consistently prove useful: a non-judgmental attitude, and a dedication to doing things the right way.

Who Am I to Judge?

Shone Evans enjoyed considerable success as a player in the 1990s at McNeese State University, in Louisiana. After his final season, he was sure he would make it to the NFL—so he didn't complete his degree. The NFL never called, though. Evans had his future taken out from under him, and worse, there was no college degree to land on.

Fortunately, Evans had a family to help him. His grandmother, both of his parents and two of his brothers were special-education teachers, and so Evans decided to go back to school and earn a degree in special education. Evans finished his degree—and he also began coaching football.

When he landed a top job at La Marque High School, Evans said he tried to be every boss he ever had. By the second year—after much trial and error—he had finally figured out who *he* was, as a leader. In the words of the Christian faith that Evans believes in so strongly, he became a servant-leader.

"Who am I to ridicule kids who make bad decisions?" asked Evans. "I left college, and I was wrong."

Instead of judging his players, Evans leads by showing up every day and in every way. "I haven't changed my phone number in 27 years," Evans says, "because my biggest fear is not being there."

Starting Over

When it comes to rebuilding the program at La Marque, Evans has left no piece unexamined.

"You can't raise kids the way we were raised," he says, "because the world we knew has changed." As a result, Evans is willing to change every part of his kids' lives.

Evans' program begins with nutrition—and, literally, with peanut butter and jelly jars. Every day, Evans makes sure that there is bread, peanut butter and jelly available in his office. Anyone—player or not—can come by, drop a quarter in a jar, and make a sandwich. At the end of the week, his wife takes the money collected, buys more supplies, and makes sure that the coach has them in his office on Monday morning.

"Our kids don't understand great nutrition," Evans says, knowing that cooking fresh foods every day is not in the cards for many of his guys. "Unfortunately, we live in a society where it's cheaper to eat McDonald's than to purchase and cook some chicken and green beans."

Evans also places a great emphasis on academics. He carries out what a lot of coaches do—grade checks, study halls—and then he goes a step beyond.

"We make our kids write down their goals, and then we work with the English teacher to make those goals read well," says Evans. In other words, it's the coach's way of trying to bridge the athletic-academic gap.

Going even further, Evans insists that all of his coaches are certified to teach.

"If a kid needs help with his homework, we'll help him. And if we can't, we'll find someone who can," he says.

Evans' goal with academics is simple: Every kid will be academically eligible for college, whether they choose to play football or not.

Then there's learning how to handle yourself.

"We teach our kids to shake hands, look the individual in the eye, and then step back," says Evans. For many adults, such skills are so second-nature that they have forgotten that they were once learned. Evans makes sure his guys learn them.

Learning to Trust

What Evans teaches most, however, is honesty. He is brutally honest with his guys, with their parents, and with the community at large. He will not promise what he cannot deliver, and he will not lead others on a path that he feels they cannot succeed at.

"Kids today don't trust," says Evans. "These kids want to know, 'What can you do for me?' That's not bad, it's just the reality."

And apparently, his methods are working.

"We can't get our kids to leave," says Evans. "When the bell rings at 4:10, we have 40 kids in our football office. Once they know how much you care, they will run through a wall with you."

The one thing Evans is very slow to do is to give up on anyone. Cutting a player, or dropping a man from the team for violations of rules, is always tough. But for Evans, it's especially so. Often, if he cuts someone loose, there is no safety net available to catch the kid.

"I've had to let a few go because they were hurting the program," says Evans, who admits that he still loses sleep over it. "When the good guys stop letting you play with them, the bad guys have a field day."

The community is learning to trust Evans, too. Last year, the team put together a winning record—and 10 of his players went on to play football at either the Division II or Division III level.

Evans is also bringing back the players from the team's "glory years."

"I invite all the guys who wore the blue and gold to come back. They are key to winning the support of La Marque," he says. "The community has to understand what you're doing."

Life in La Marque is no vacation—but then, Coach Evans isn't selling exotic dreams. He's building his players for the future, and in the process, is restoring pride and hope in his town.

24

Ben Gucciardi

"If it's all about winning, you're undervaluing the potential of it and the value of the work."

Soccer

Founder: Soccer Without Borders

Oakland International High School (2007–present)

Ben Gucciardi is a different breed of coach. Many of us are evangelists for the transformative power of sports and coaches in a young person's life, but how many of us think about the issue of access? It's one thing to touch the lives of kids who come to you, but how does one touch the lives of kids who may benefit from what you do, but can't get to you? Perhaps there are limited spots on the team; perhaps these kids are financially unable to participate; perhaps they're simply not comfortable stepping out on their own, for fear of ridicule or being embarrassed in front of their peers.

Gucciardi works with immigrant children—the group of individuals that quite possibly faces the most barriers to sports access in the U.S. Gucciardi is working to crack the issue of access with these children, and in so doing is offering a new way of thinking about sports in America.

Gucciardi is best known for his work as the founder of Soccer Without Borders, an international nonprofit with programs in five U.S. cities, Nicaragua and Uganda. He's also a high school coach at Oakland International High School. Here, we explore how Gucciardi faced countless issues related to access and built a program that is truly available to anyone who wants to take part.

For a lucky few, sports are a ticket out—out of poverty, out of a tough home life, out of a dysfunctional community.

Ben Gucciardi didn't need a ticket out. He did, however, grow up in San Francisco and frequently find himself the odd person out. On his travel soccer team, Gucciardi was usually the only Anglo—and Spanish, not English, was the language of choice. Further, many of his teammates were immigrants.

Rather than fear those different from him, Gucciardi welcomed and loved his teammates. "That was my community," he says.

Soccer ultimately took Gucciardi away from his community. Following high school, Gucciardi attended Lehigh University, an elite private university in Pennsylvania. There, he starred on the soccer team and served as captain of the Mountain Hawks' nationally ranked program.

Gucciardi's Bay Area community never left him, though. During the summers, he returned home and worked with Hispanic immigrants in the city's Mission District, as part of a youth sports program. While the work was enjoyable for Gucciardi, he was starting to become more aware of just how daunting life in America can truly be for immigrant children.

His girlfriend (wife) is the one who opened his eyes. Working for the International Rescue Committee—an organization that assists in refugee resettlement by supporting families looking for housing and work—she got him thinking differently about soccer, about coaching, and about sports.

A Common Thread, a Path Forward

As a talented athlete and a highly recruited player, Gucciardi had a fairly typical experience with soccer in high school and on his travel team. "For me growing up," he said, "it was always about the sport first."

As his wife began to help him understand not only the problems that immigrant kids face once they're in the U.S., but also the trauma they often endure before ever arriving, Gucciardi came to a stark realization: While there are a number of places that offer free, accessible soccer programs for kids, the *real* issue is the barriers that keep many of the kids from taking part.

To address the barriers issue, Gucciardi and his wife started a summer soccer program for refugees. Many of the kids who participated that inaugural year had experienced a significant amount of trauma just in getting to America. The program's primary focus was breaking down barriers to participation, but it also offered soccer instruction, assistance with school and help with any other issue that the kids faced.

Coincidentally, during the same summer that the program was launched, a new school was opening in Oakland, California, that was aimed specifically at educating immigrant children. The principal became aware of Gucciardi's camp and asked to see how he might work with Oakland International High School, to help its students transition to life in America.

A Different Starting Point

Starting a soccer program at Oakland International High School (OIHS) proved to be a challenge fraught with problems. The academic shortcomings of the students were substantial, and while the language barrier was the most obvious hurdle, it was far from the only one.

Many of the students at OIHS experienced "interrupted educations": They may have received schooling in their native countries, but their journey to America led them through immigration camps where no education was available. So, while a student might be eligible for ninth grade according to their age, a disruption in their education caused them to miss grades 7 and 8.

Immigrant students also do not frequently have the comfort of a safety net. Many of the children leave school to work the 4 p.m. to midnight shift at a low-paying, menial job that their family needs in order to stay afloat.

Finally, many of these kids faced substantial trauma in getting to the United States. Whether in their homeland, their migrant camps or their new neighborhood, these children had seen and experienced life in ways that most middle-class Americans simply can't imagine.

The net effect of these problems meant that a traditional approach to soccer simply wouldn't work. Consider, for example, the incentives that many coaches use to motivate high school players: no-show, no-play; poor grades get someone kicked off the team. These incentives simply do not work at OIHS.

So Gucciardi built a nontraditional structure. There would be no varsity, junior varsity or freshman teams. He began with a boys' team and a girls' team. Games were played on Saturdays, and during the week, Gucciardi and his other coaches would work with team members on their assignments.

If a student wasn't making grades or attending, it wasn't a signal to coaches to look elsewhere. It was a red flag that that student needed additional support. "If the kid is putting forth the effort but can't hold a 2.0 GPA," says Gucciardi, "it's not a barrier."

Word of the team caught on quickly, and soon, more kids wanted to join. Rather than limiting who could play, Gucciardi simply created more teams. If his players had friends at other high schools who wanted to get involved, he made room for them, too.

A Change in Coaching

No one at Oakland International High School is kidding themselves: They realize that they aren't raising the next Lionel Messi or creating a program that's going to rack up reams of regional and sectional championships.

"We begin from an entirely different perspective about what sport is," Gucciardi says. "We see sport as a container that creates space where the kids can be themselves and connect with others and get support."

Rather than winning being the focus, Gucciardi and his coaches find success in getting students to the field—especially the girls, who often come from environments that discourage them from getting involved in sports.

Even the program's mantras are atypical. Instead of phrases that promote aggressiveness on the field, these teams' chants are framed to create a safe space. The coaches live by the mantra, "Get them to the field." The players are constantly met with expressions such as, "Glad that you're here!" and, "Leave your shoes at the door."

Gucciardi's goal is to get his players out of their shells and to try.

"These kids have had a pretty intense journey to get here," says Gucciardi. "Some don't want to talk to people. They are in their own world.

[But] there's a therapeutic element to play. The kids can be themselves, reconnect to different parts of themselves. Your job, as a coach, is to do the outreach and try and get these people to come."

The approach is working. The program continues to grow, and the school recently opened its own soccer field. The idea and push to build this field came, coincidentally, from the students themselves. Many of the teams now compete in travel leagues, and one team competes in the interscholastic league. The focus of Gucciardi's work, however, hasn't changed.

His goal is still to remove barriers to accessing sport. The real question, in Gucciardi's mind, is simple: Why aren't we all doing this?

Part V:
Developing a
Coaching Philosophy

"If you just take off some of the pressure, sometimes things happen easier because somebody believes in you."
—Gail Maundrell

25

Gail Maundrell

"If you just take off some of the pressure, sometimes things happen easier because somebody believes in you."

Gymnastics, tennis

Head coach: Turpin High School (1975–present)

When coach Gail Maundrell was in high school, she was a majorette. She had no choice, after all: During her teenage years there was no Title IX, and very few options were available for female athletes. Maundrell did have a role model, though: a sixth grade teacher whom she so admired that she chose to attend Ball State University, her teacher's alma mater.

As a student at Ball State University, Gail Maundrell was a four-sport athlete: she took part in gymnastics, field hockey, swimming and diving, and tennis. Neither Maundrell nor the women she played alongside were recruited athletes, though; they simply enjoyed sports and learned together. Years later, that desire to compete and the love of sport is still with Maundrell—and while Maundrell's appreciation for athletics hasn't changed over time, the world of women's sports has changed dramatically.

Today, high school-aged athletes who compete in the sports Maundrell coaches—tennis and gymnastics—can earn college scholarships. The competition to earn those scholarships is fierce, and training starts very early. To get kids on that track, club sports—sometimes called "travel" sports, or "pay-to-play" sports—have surged. Parents enroll their kids in high-quality (and often high-pressure) training at ages as young as 3 or 4.

Years later, the best athletes are drawn to club sports, and colleges now recruit directly out of clubs—not high schools.

While these club teams thrive, high school gymnastics has struggled. High cost, the large amount of space required to have a team, a lack of quality coaches—all has taken a toll. In the district where Maundrell coaches, these pressures have lowered the number of gymnastics teams from 55, in 1975, to just 16. Where some may see trouble, though, Maundrell sees opportunity.

An Honest Broker

Coach Maundrell knows the score and doesn't promise what she can't deliver.

"I tell my girls: If you were going to the Olympics, then you wouldn't be here for me to talk to, so let's focus on getting better and having fun along the way."

A big part of that fun is the theme that Maundrell selects each year. On the surface, some themes may seem a bit out of step with a high school gymnastics program.

"One of my favorites was Dr. Seuss. I have a big hat that I wear, and we used expressions like 'One flip, two flip, you flip, I flip,'" says Maundrell. "Competing schools enjoy it, too. Every year, they're asking, 'What's your theme for next year?'"

Behind the fun and the silliness, though, is a lot of hard work and commitment.

"I don't like to lose, but in individual sports like gymnastics, you're going to lose," says Maundrell. "Celebrate the positives and get over the negatives. If you dwell on those, you're only going to be worse."

Maundrell has a more succinct way of conveying her message to kids who complain about judges or gripe when the training gets too hard: "SIU." Or, "Suck it up."

Skills are at the heart of Maundrell's teaching, as is learning to acquire them safely. With the rise of club sports has come a dramatic rise in injuries to young athletes—and Maundrell knows where the problem lies. "Every sport has gone to year-round. I see little kids at 10 years old tearing their ACLs," she says. "A lot of them just get burned out. They get to high school, and they just don't want to do it anymore."

At Turpin High School, gymnastics is a four-month program; the tennis season spans two months. Maundrell's athletes master skills and have a record of winning at the district and state levels, but what Maundrell values more is that, at the end of the season, the girls' bodies are intact. This is not to say that injuries don't happen—gymnastics, like any sport, carries risk of bodily harm—but by limiting training time and not relentlessly pushing kids year-round to drive higher, harder and faster, Turpin's gymnasts stay relatively healthy.

More to the point, they learn. Notes Maundrell, "If you just take off some of the pressure, sometimes things happen easier because somebody believes in you."

Bottom Line:
I'm Training Them for Life, not Their Sport

The idea that Maundrell's approach works is hardly in dispute. In fact, she has regularly had gymnasts leave club teams to join her high school team—and love it.

Maundrell probably won't grow Olympic gymnasts, but with just a few individuals making the Olympic team every four years, there's a lot of wisdom in her approach. "Taking a kid from being able to do nothing to doing a simple beam routine is really something that sticks with you," she says. And it sticks with her athletes, too.

Today, at 70 years old, what Maundrell is most struck by is the impact she has had on so many lives. Former athletes introduce her to their children; former students stop her in the street and talk about the experiences they had with her. Oftentimes, she doesn't remember the individual experiences. It's not an insult to the individual, but just a testimony to how many athletes she has influenced.

"After so many years, the really talented ones stick out and the troublemakers you remember," she says. "But the good kids, well, there's so many of them."

Perhaps one of these years she'll sit back and gather her scrapbooks, and remember them all. But right now, she has more important things to do. Her tennis program is growing in popularity, with 28 girls going out for the team.

More lives to touch. The memories can wait.

26

Phil 'Smokey' Moresi

*"I needed leaders on my second team and my
bench that would make things happen."*

Basketball

Head coach: Framington South High School

*The hard reality of high school sports is that players are now at a level
where they must learn to accept their limitations. Love of the game simply
isn't enough if your core skills are lacking or your physical attributes don't
measure up. For many, the mental resilience necessary to play at a higher
level is just too much.*

*Those who can't break the starting lineup are often derided because they
don't share the spotlight. Coach Phil "Smokey" Moresi, however, took those
who lacked the God-given talents of his best athletes and turned them into
something else: leaders. Leaders whom, even the starters found, they couldn't
do without.*

So many of the words and phrases we use to describe successful coaches
are cliché: "fiery," "smart," "disciplined," "intense." The terms are accurate,
but they have a way of creating caricatures—and Phil "Smokey" Moresi is
no caricature. He's an American original.

Talk with the people who know him, and all the clichés fit. The athletic director at Ashland High School, where Moresi spent his final three
years coaching the girls' varsity basketball team, calls him "fiery." David
Blatt, former head coach of the Cleveland Cavaliers and considered by

some the smartest basketball mind in the game, says that the lessons he learned from Moresi during his high school years were the most important lessons in his development—and that's high praise from a man who played under legendary coach Pete Carril at Princeton. Howard Brown, a successful technology entrepreneur who also played for Moresi, describes him as "Bill Belichek before Bill Belichek" because of the intense, disciplined approach that Moresi brought to the game.

These descriptions capture the coach that people saw on the sidelines for decades, but they don't capture Moresi's true genius: how he approached teaching the game of basketball. To understand that, you've got to look at what today's fans derisively call the "benchwarmers," or the "scrubs."

Second-team Leadership

For Phil Moresi, the second team was a significant key to success—and key to his long string of wins and championships at Framington South. Like all coaches, he counted on his second team to run the opposition's plays in practice so that the starters were ready on game day. Moresi wanted these second stringers to be much more than sparring partners, though. He wanted them to be leaders, as well.

"Of course I had great players who were outstanding leaders and role models for our program, but I needed leaders on my second team and my bench that would make things happen," said Moresi. "[Their] leadership was just as important … as the best player on the team."

This "second-team leadership" played out in several key areas, but it was most evident on the practice court.

During the 1970s—in the heyday of Framington South basketball—just about the only sound one would hear in the gym during practice was the squeak of Converse tennis shoes, as feet slid across the waxed court. This was accompanied by the occasional grunts that followed player collisions and the call of plays and switches by team leaders.

Moresi didn't lead practice, so much as orchestrate it. He would post a schedule each day for the players to learn and follow, and they would carry out that schedule to a T—largely in silence, under the watchful eyes of Moresi and his associates. This approach forced everyone to take responsibility for their own role and to execute it to perfection. In other words, in Moresi's practices, the second-team members were not second-rate; instead, they made up the engine that drove the team.

It helped that Moresi leveraged his second team's competitive juices. As he recalls, the second team often worked the starters harder in practice than opponents worked them on game nights. Since the second team worked so hard, Moresi says that it helped the starters score points quicker on game night. "The second team then would get into the game quicker," he says.

And if the second team didn't perform well in the game?

"There were times that the second team went in, and things didn't go very well, and we'd watch a 17-point lead dissipate," says Moresi. "The first-teamers would get nervous and get itchy to get in. I would say, 'No. We're going into the locker at the half with whatever lead the second team gives us.'"

This led to the first-team players working the second-team players harder in practice over the next two or three days.

In short, iron was sharpening iron.

Beyond the Game

There's a case to be made that Moresi trusted his second team more than he did his first team. These benchwarmers had to execute their job to perfection in order for the starting team to execute their best on game nights. Moresi also needed these players to work hard so that he could focus on his other task: getting his starters recruited.

Today's recruiting game is so hyper-charged that it's hard to imagine how different it was in the 1970s.

"At that time there was no video or travel," Moresi says. There were no "showcase" events that brought 100 coaches to watch the performance of 50 of the best athletes in a region. There was no video that players could upload and send to college coaches. There was no email, either, so most players couldn't even entertain the thought of talking to a college coach. Instead, coaches came to the schools.

"Every night in my gym, I had five to seven Division I head coaches or assistant coaches watching practice," says Moresi. The coach trusted his second stringers to execute their jobs, to keep practice moving quickly and to make everyone work harder, because this gave the coaches the good looks they came for. It also gave Moresi the time to advocate for those he knew could play at the collegiate level.

If the backups were setting the platform for the starters *on* the court, they were also the leaders in the school *off* the court—and more people were starting to notice.

"The second teamers were able to develop their own leadership qualities: A guy might be the last on the team's depth chart, but he would put the work into class and be rewarded by his teacher for that effort," says Moresi. "That motivated the others in the class with him. We got great reports back from all of our teachers on 85% to 90% of our players."

Always Growing

Moresi's approach to second-team players isn't something that he suddenly hit upon, but rather something that emerged over his years in the profession. Moresi started in 1968 as an assistant coach, and during that time he traveled around the region, watching others and learning the game. Among those Moresi watched was a young Bobby Knight at West Point, and his senior point guard Mike Krzyzewski—two people who would become giants in the world of college basketball. (Knight at Indiana University, three NCAA National Championships; and Krzyzewski at Duke University, five NCAA National Championships). Moresi admired the way they ran practice, and how hard every member of the team had to work. He also learned by watching practice at nearby Boston College.

"I would monitor BC's off-season workouts and give little check marks on who was working hard and who wasn't working hard," he said. "I would take my teams in to watch college practices. Watching how hard their second teams worked, I just sort of put that together. It was an easy way to work with people."

Today, Moresi often speaks with young coaches about his approach to the game—about the importance of drills, about building a solid second team. Unfortunately, his advice isn't utilized in the way it once was.

"They're receptive," he says, "but I go watch them later, and nothing has changed." They can't change, he says, because "that style of play isn't fast enough for today's players."

Perhaps. But coaches can certainly learn from the master about how important it is to not just *say* that they value every player, but to *show* them.

The results of such efforts take years to bubble up—but, emerge they do.

Like on a fall evening in Cleveland in 2014. Just before David Blatt was about to coach his first game as a head coach in the NBA, he sent a text to Moresi just as the national anthem was about to play: "Thanks for getting me here, Coach."

27

Phil 'Smokey' Moresi, from Howard Brown

"You busted your butt, even though you knew you may not play. That allowed you to develop the resiliency and the skills to move on through life."

—Howard Brown

Basketball

Head coach: Framington South High School

There is a hard edge to coaching. In the grand scheme of things, the games we play are just that—games. But to be great at those games requires tenacity, extreme attention to detail and a relentless pursuit of perfection. As the great Vince Lombardi said, "We won't achieve perfection … but in striving for it, we perhaps will find excellence." Some coaches take this too far, forgetting that they are working with young people. But great coaches know that toughness, balanced with respect and appreciation, builds character and resilience for the very real game of life. I have known Howard Brown for a little more than five years now, and his life is a testament to the power of positive influence that a coach—one who balances toughness with love—can have on those who play for him or her.

July 4, 2020: The short video clip on Howard Brown's Facebook page shows a middle-aged man wearing a Babson College basketball jersey, dribbling from the top of the key toward the basket—stopping and popping, from 15 feet away. His parting words?

"That's how we do it. I want to wish everyone a happy July Fourth. Be safe … put on a mask … cancer sucks."

Brown has survived cancer not once, but twice. The first time, at age 24, it was stage 4e Non-Hodgkin lymphoma. A bone marrow transplant from his twin sister, performed in May of 1990, saved his life. The second time, Brown was diagnosed with stage 3 colorectal cancer. It was June of 2016, and Brown saw the disease advance to stage 4 metastatic cancer—and lived to tell the tale.

Brown is currently penning a book about his life called *Shining Brightly*, and anyone who knows him understands that the person who built his foundation—and sparked a light that keeps him burning brightly—is his high school basketball coach, Phil "Smokey" Moresi.

A Star Takes Many Shapes

What Brown appreciates most about Moresi is not what he learned while leading the high school team as the starting point guard his senior year. No, it's the lessons Moresi taught him the preceding three years, when he either wasn't on the varsity team or was sitting on the bench.

Howard could have started on a lot of teams his junior year, but Steve Niccoli—the returning starting point guard—was a senior.

"We went 6-12 that year," Brown says. "Niccoli won the MVP of the Bay State League for a team with a losing record."

Niccoli had to earn every minute of his playing time, though, because in spite of the fact that Brown wasn't playing, he was riding Niccoli the whole year—in practice.

That effort didn't go unnoticed by Moresi, who pulled Brown aside at the year's end. "Howard, I got to tell you, the reason Stevie won that award was because you were so good that you pushed him," said Moresi, "and [you] became a pain in his ass."

Brown took it as the highest possible compliment.

"[Moresi] knew that being second-team was really difficult," Brown says. "You busted your butt, even though you knew you may not play."

What Brown could only partially appreciate at the time was how important that second-team lesson would be.

BEEF

Just how much Howard would come to depend on those skills was something that he could not know at the tender ages of 17 and 18. He couldn't see the two bouts with cancer in his future; he couldn't see the ups and downs of being a serial entrepreneur, an interfaith leader, and a cancer survivor/advocate.

Today, some 40 years after Brown last dribbled a ball on his high school court, the lessons that Coach Moresi taught are still with him—for example, how to shoot a free throw.

"For foul shots, he taught us BEEF," Brown says. It's an acronym for:

Balance
Elbow-in
Eyes on the rim
Follow through

Such a skill is certainly important in basketball, but is it in life?

When Brown was facing cancer for the second time, he used BEEF to fight for his health and life.

If he were to fight, Brown knew that he had to do four things:

First, he had to maintain his **balance**. Writing about his struggle with cancer in an article for Read the Spirit, Brown said, "We learn to lean on others, to depend on others—and eventually to reach out and let others lean on us, depend on us."

For many of us, leaning on others is a sign of weakness. For Howard, learning to lean on others was simply a way to maintain balance in his struggle.

Second, he had to keep **elbow-in**. When shooting a basketball, it's natural to let your elbow fly out. Learning to control it, keeping it tucked in, is the secret to consistently making shots. It keeps the ball flight straight and produces the proper arc. Through numerous bouts of chemo and four major surgeries, Brown kept his elbow in. He was doing the difficult mental work of just waking up every morning and doing what had to be done, even when his body had other ideas.

Third, he had to keep his **eyes on the rim**. The goal was beating cancer via laser focus and mental toughness. "Eyes on the rim" is the visualization of the basketball swishing through the net. Brown could not allow an air of defeat to distract him from his goal. Death was, of course, a very real possibility. Along the way Brown had met and then lost many friends and acquaintances who were also struggling with cancer. None he met, however, took their eyes off the rim.

Fourth, he had to **follow through**. Now ranked among the lucky colorectal cancer survivors, Howard has become a national advocate, spokesperson and leader in the fight against this dreaded disease. He frequently reminds everyone to get screened, in efforts to prevent colorectal cancer.

Fiery

Today, when Brown talks about his old coach, "fiery" is a term that inevitably comes up. After all, Moresi was tough. He would get into it with the referees. And, yes, he would even sometimes get thrown out of games.

Yet it was that fieriness that drove Moresi and his players to keep striving, to keep improving—whether they were undefeated and hoisting state championship trophies or fighting through 6-12 seasons.

It's the little things, in sports—the little things that great coaches drill into their young players—that stick with them.

At 18, BEEF was Howard Brown's world. The fate of the universe, as the great former UCLA star Bill Walton once said, hung in the balance when that ball was in your hands.

Forty years on, BEEF still affects Brown's world. The great lessons are hard-learned—over, and over, and over again.

"That's how we do it … cancer sucks."

28

Adam Cook

"I tell these young coaches, 'You're my hero. You're the ones making a difference. Changing lives.'"

Football

Head coach: Whitehouse High School 2013–2017

Athletic director: Whitehouse High School 2018–present

There is something charmingly disarming about Adam Cook. He bristles a bit when talking about coaching because people best know him as the man who coached Patrick Mahomes—arguably the most exciting player in the NFL since Brett Favre. Cook isn't comfortable with the attention this has brought him. Yes, Mahomes is a great story, and Cook understands why people are interested in their relationship. But, he notes, so are the other kids at Whitehouse High School who are changing the world by becoming doctors and missionaries and lawyers and artists. Make no mistake—Cook loves coaching and football. But it all falls apart without raising a community of people who know who they are, and how to work together for the common good. That's how Cook approaches football. That's how he approaches life.

Adam Cook's first coaching job was at a middle school in Daingerfield, Texas—a town of only about 2,500 people. That year, he watched with the rest of the nation as two jetliners crashed into the World Trade Center towers, a third crashed into the Pentagon, and a fourth nose-dived into a field in Pennsylvania before it could reach its destination—presumably the United States Capitol.

"That's the day sports just sort of stood still," Cook recalls. In the days that followed, his only concern was to help his young charges on the team and in his science classrooms to make sense of what was happening.

"I shared with those kids the mindset of those who were serving in the armed forces," Cook recalls. "I felt the weight of responsibility to teach them what is right and wrong. To help them understand that you've got to stand for something in this life, and you have to know what you are going to stand for and why."

That's been what coaching and life has been about for Cook ever since.

We Are the Daingerfield Tigers!

The town of Daingerfield has never left Coach Cook. It is, in many ways, his coaching foundation, and he reaches back to those years constantly when talking about working with young athletes and football.

Life there can be tough. Many folks work in the steel industry. It's a place where people can't afford to turn on one another, and it's a place where people know what they stand for. What really seems to have affected Cook, however, is the town's commitment to working together toward a common goal. Whatever that goal might be.

"I couldn't have asked for a better community to be involved with," Cook says. "Hardworking families who know what has to be done and just find a way to do it."

In short, this is a community that pulls together and works hard to do what needs to be done. Perhaps nothing summed up the dogged, blue-collar character of Daingerfield's residents better than a scrappy, smallish offensive guard on Cook's junior high school team.

"We were down by two touchdowns with less than two minutes to play in one game," Cook recalls, and this little kid steps up to rally his troops and says, "Man, we're the Daingerfield Tigers, we're not out of this yet.'"

That determination. That sense of self and community. That roll-up-your-sleeves-and-get-to-work mentality. That is what Cook has taught for two decades.

Sparks Fly

Traumatic events like September 11, 2001, have a way of bringing clarity to individuals and communities about who they are and what really matters in life. That clarity can be short-lived, however, as life returns to normalcy. Those lessons must be constantly re-learned.

To teach these, Cook leans heavily on his Christian faith. Among the biblical verses that Cook is fond of comes from the book of Proverbs. "As iron sharpens iron, so one person sharpens another."

"Sharpening iron can be ugly," Cook says. "Sparks fly. You're going to get frustrated, things are going to happen. But if we can keep the same goal ... Live a sacrificial life. The key to getting anywhere is to serve others."

That's what Cook learned from the guard at Daingerfield. And it's a lesson that would later help him launch the still-rising star of Super Bowl Champion quarterback of the Kansas City Chiefs, Patrick Mahomes.

When Cook was coaching him, Mahomes was special, but his playing style raised more questions than accolades at first. "Patrick was such a unique player," Cook says. "Not everyone was for him at first. Receivers had to get used to a play never being dead with him, and changing the way they ran routes and broke-off routes."

At the time, Mahomes was competing with Ryan Cheatham for the starting QB job. Cheatham was a more-classic-style player. A player with all the attributes college scouts look for.

The battle between the two is the type that often tears teams apart. Players favoring one quarterback over another and losing sight of the common goal. To avoid that, Cook sat the two young men down and had both read Tony Dungy's book *Uncommon*. "We talked about the characteristics of the uncommon man," Cook said. "Cheatham decided to come back and play receiver and not QB," Cook said. "That's character."

Mahomes, Cook notes, appreciated Cheatham, and his other receivers, too. "Patrick couldn't have done it without those other guys," Cook says. "And he knows and appreciates that."

Our Coaches Across America Are in A Fight

As this chapter is being written, the nation is again at a stop. This time it's the Covid-19 pandemic that has stalled life. It's also a period where people are surfacing deeply rooted issues around race and raising issues that are again unsettling the national fabric. Whereas some see strife in these factors, Cook finds something more important. An opportunity to more clearly see ourselves and our communities. Just as happened in Daingerfield.

The difference is today he is an athletic director, not a coach. So instead of teaching players, he's working with and empowering coaches to do this important work in these trying days.

"Our coaches across America are in a fight," Cook says. "My role now is to encourage those coaches to remind those kids of the platform that they have. I tell these young coaches, 'You're my hero. You're the ones making a difference. Changing lives.'"

One of his heroes is head football coach Marcus Gold. "Our kids need to be in front of Coach Gold," Cook says. Gold, who is biracial, has become a leader at school in healing the racial divide that continues to haunt our nation. In a school roughly equally split along racial lines, "having a head coach who sees that struggle, and who brings his unique perspective," is important. "It's an honor to have him," says Cook.

He knows the hard discussions are worth it. They are painful at times in the present, but down the road we all reap the benefits. "When I see Patrick Mahomes come out and take the stand he has taken on Black Lives Matter," Cook says, "it's inspiring."

At the end of the day, Cook has come to appreciate that everyone has to "surrender to the process and give up the outcome." The process is learning what you stand for, and learning to pull together toward a common goal. The outcomes? They're not wins and losses. They're the sentiments of a young, scrappy player in the small town of Daingerfield. "We're the Tigers! And we're not out of this thing yet!"

29

George Stackhouse

"You don't have to be a millionaire, but you can be successful and give back to your community."

Men's Basketball

Head coach: Westover High School (2007–present), Kinston High School (1999–2001)

Basketball in North Carolina is approached with all the passion of wrestling in Iowa and football in Texas. George Stackhouse has become a giant in the Tarheel State's world of high school hoops. This fact was recognized in 2020 when the Associated Press named him All-State Coach of the Year. What's notable about Stackhouse, however, is where he's climbed these heights. Not in a well-financed private school, or some of the wealthier high schools in Charlotte, Greensboro, Raleigh, or Wilmington. Rather, he's done this at Westover High School in Fayetteville. In this piece, Stackhouse talks about the opportunities his kids have, and the importance of community both on the court and after one's playing days are done.

Don't talk to Coach George Stackhouse about the disadvantages his kids face.

Yes, he coaches at a school where 100 percent of the student population receives free and reduced-price lunch. Yes, many of his kids come from broken homes. Yes, most of his kids have never had anyone in their families go to college.

"We don't use our situation as a crutch." It's not the disadvantages, after all, that he focuses on as a coach. It's the opportunities. Throughout his life, Stackhouse has had—and taken full advantage of—the opportunities the game has given him. In his journey one can see the road he lays before his athletes.

Lucky to Be in the Game

Stackhouse grew up on a farm in Fairmont, North Carolina. Located in the eastern part of the state not too far from the South Carolina border, it's a town whose name people mostly likely know because they see it on signs along I-95 as they drive south to Florida for vacation. Poverty is high, and sports are a form of escape.

He grew up a multisport athlete. He was All-State in football, All-County in baseball. His high school baseball team won a state championship in 1986. Ironically, in the sport that he is now best known for—basketball— he describes himself as "marginal." After high school he made his way to East Carolina University where he graduated in 1991.

His coaching career started at Fairmont High School, where he was an assistant and was part of another state championship team. In 1998 he became the first, and so far only, head basketball coach at Kinston High School. His team lost the state title game in 2001—his last year at Kinston.

For the next several years, he was an assistant coach at his college alma mater. East Carolina is part of Conference USA. Not a Power Five school, but the coaches in that conference would go on to define the world of major college basketball. His Pirates teams went against Rick Pitino at Louisville, Mike Anderson at the University of Alabama at Birmingham, John Calipari at Memphis, and Tom Crean at Marquette.

The pull of high school basketball, however, brought him to Fayetteville. He's been at Westover since 2008.

He feels lucky to be in the game, and he never takes what the game has given him for granted. He expects the same of every young man who plays for him.

A Demanding Culture

"I put my players first. At the end of the day, there is nothing that I wouldn't do for them to keep them successful," says Stackhouse.

In return, however, he expects his players to work. Hard. "We don't stress a victim type of approach to life. We want winners. We get kids in difficult situations at home. But even there, there are opportunities when you can grab hold."

Everything begins with honest conversations. High schools can only carry so many players on their rosters—usually around 15. Stackhouse is straight-up with his players about where they stand. They are lucky to be where they are, and they have opportunities they can grab. Take advantage of the team, however, and you'll find yourself on the outside looking in.

Stackhouse recalls one player who, skill-wise, was by far the best player on his team. Character-wise, however, he simply wasn't doing it in school. Stackhouse took the kid off the team for the entirety of his junior year.

The young man returned his senior year and won the team leadership award.

Another young man was not allowed to play in a playoff game because he was late arriving to the bus.

"I'm not in it for state titles," Stackhouse says. "I'm really in it to see the guys make goals and reach them to be successful in life." Sometimes, it takes removing a kid from the program to make them understand how to reach for goals and be successful.

"We are a demanding culture. But the kids will rise to our standards. We expect them to be role models in our school."

To ask this much of his players, Stackhouse knows that he must ask even more of himself.

"I'm a lot different coach than I was even 10 years ago," he says. "You constantly have to adapt to motivate them."

Perhaps most important, Stackhouse says: "I hold myself most accountable for everything. Seeing them improve, seeing them grow as people, those are the biggest things. There's no tiring with that."

Pride in Community

Growing as people and achieving goals does not go hand-in-hand with forgetting where one is from. It's tempting when working at a high-poverty school to measure success by how many leave and go on to better things.

Not so with Stackhouse. "A measuring stick for me is the number of players who come back and want to be part of the program after they've gone."

One can argue that it's the most important measure of success for Stackhouse. When his kids move on from high school, they move on with self-confidence and a sense of pride about who they are and where they came from. They also move on with a sense of responsibility to help those around them.

"You don't have to be a millionaire," Stackhouse tells his players, "but you can be successful and give back to your community."

And come back they do. As assistant coaches, as role models, and as friends.

Stackhouse calls what he instills in his players a "victorious kind of mindset." Whether you're playing basketball, or making your way through life, he teaches his kids that "it's not easy, it's going to take a lot, and you're going to have some setbacks."

Economic disadvantages are real. The road to success, however, is long. Those who make it to the end do so because they know their goals and do the hard work to reach them.

Stackhouse shows his kids day in and day out what this looks like. He lives it. "At no point do I let my standards drop in terms of what I expect from myself and from them."

The opportunities are there. If you're willing to do the work.

30

Coach Al Fracassa, from Kevin Hart

"My biggest mission as the freshman coach was to get these young men to be good friends with each other and to trust each other."

—Al Fracassa

Football

Al Fracassa
Head coach: Royal Oak Shrine Football (1960–1968), Brother Rice High School (1969–2013)

Kevin Hart
Player: Brother Rice, Notre Dame (1977–1980)
Coach: Brother Rice (2007–2015)

Kevin Hart is from football royalty. His father won the Heisman Award as a player at Notre Dame and several NFL Championships with the Detroit Lions. He sent his son to Brother Rice so he could play for Al Fracassa. From there, he went on to Notre Dame, where he won a national championship playing with Joe Montana. In this chapter, Hart reflects on how Fracassa guided his young life, and what that taught him about coaching.

Respect is one of those ethereal characteristics that great leaders have, yet people struggle to explain or teach. All coaches need the respect of their players. High school coaches, however, must also garner the respect of parents. It is one of the greatest challenges of coaching at this level.

Al Fracassa had parents' respect. There are many things one can point to that explain how he managed to garner it. Certainly winning helps. In Fracassa's 44 years at Brother Rice, he had only one losing season.

Being recognized as a brilliant coach also helps. He had multiple opportunities to take coaching positions at leading football powerhouses like Notre Dame and Michigan State. And no less a legend than Tom Landry of the Dallas Cowboys praised Fracassa's innate understanding of the passing game. Kevin Hart recalls that Landry invited the coach to speak with his staff about the mechanics and details of quarterbacking.

"Coach Fracassa was always so humble about his coaching abilities. In fact, he was one of the most innovative and progressive offensive coaches in the game," according to Hart. "He had an uncanny ability to adjust his offense to match up (or down) to his players' abilities."

For Hart, however, the key to the respect Fracassa enjoyed from his players' and their parents grew from the mindset that Fracassa instilled in his players. "The players all knew how lucky they were to be guided by this man. When he spoke, every player froze in their place so that they wouldn't miss anything. You could hear a pin drop. Just like when I played in the '70s, these boys never wanted to disappoint him. They never wanted to let him down."

Family Football Tradition

Kevin Hart is in a unique position to understand how much respect Fracassa got from everyone. Kevin's father, Leon Hart, was arguably the most dominant football player of the 1940s and 1950s. As a student-athlete at Notre Dame, Hart was a part of three national championship teams (1946, '47, and '49) and he won both the Heisman Trophy and the Maxwell Trophy in 1949. As a member of the NFL's Detroit Lions, he won three NFL Championships (1952, 1953, and 1957).

Kevin Hart had an outstanding career himself. He was part of a national championship team at Notre Dame in 1977, where he played alongside legendary quarterback Joe Montana.

Before donning the storied gold helmet, however, he wore the orange colors of Brother Rice High School and played for Fracassa. His name and pedigree, however, bought him no favors with Coach.

Kevin Hart was forced to face that reality head on, and he certainly had his doubts about sticking with football. It was the early '70s, and long hair, individualism, and anti-authoritarianism were in. Fracassa was all about loyalty, humility and unselfishness. "At the time, everyone was afraid to tell us what to do," Hart said. "Not Al Fracassa. He told us exactly what to do. It's exactly what we needed."

He was able to ask so much, however, because "he stressed that every player was vital to the success of the team," Hart recalls. "Every player felt the heavy responsibility. There was not a single player who could miss a practice or a team meeting without him being on top of it. He would know if you were distracted or unfocused. He wanted the commitment to be to each teammate." That meant short hair, self-discipline and playing the position where your team needed you most. It also meant knowing your role with the team and behaving like a gentleman—with the starters, scout team members, water boy or the opposition.

You Talk with Your Parents

This singular focus on players being 100 percent committed to their teammates is at the heart of how Fracassa earned the respect of parents.

In the same way that Fracassa expected his players to express any concerns they had about how they were, or were not, being played to the coaches, he expected his players to deal with their parents if they complained about the program or their son's playing time. "We all knew who was supposed to be on the field," Hart said. If the parents had a problem, "it was the player's responsibility to let them know what we know in this group." Playing time is earned, not given.

Players embraced this to the point that if "your parents came in to talk with Fracassa, it was embarrassing," according to Hart. "There was an unspoken rule that you did not want your parents to fight your battles."

Early in his career when he was frustrated, Hart would complain to his famous father. Leon Hart, however, had complete faith in Coach Fracassa. "If I came home and was complaining about something, my dad would look at me, and simply say: 'Figure out what he wants, and when you figure it out, you give it to him.'"

Carrying on the Tradition

That time with Coach Fracassa shaped every aspect of Kevin Hart's life. As a young man, he credits Fracassa with keeping him on the straight and narrow, and not getting drawn into the influences that could have led him down a far less productive path. "Fracassa is such a great example of how to live a good life. How to be a good father, a good husband and especially a good friend. He will help players he coached 30 years ago through their tougher challenges in life."

Further, Hart owes his career at Notre Dame to Fracassa. "Early on I thought I was a basketball player, but I wasn't," Hart says. He had hoped to attend the University of Detroit where Dick Vitale was the coach at the time. "However," Hart continues, "Al knew that I needed to play football, and that playing at Notre Dame was my best path for success."

When Hart went to Notre Dame to attend a basketball camp, Fracassa arranged for him to meet the offensive line coach, Brian Boulac, at the school. "I didn't want to do it, but I did it out of respect for Coach Fracassa. That put me on their radar."

Finally, in 2007, Hart got the chance to give some back to the man who'd given him so much.

"He asked me to be the freshman coach. He said just a year or two, until he retires. I said I'd have to talk to my wife first." Little did Hart know, Fracassa has already beat him to it. "I already spoke with her," Fracassa told Hart, "she said it was fine." So, for the next nine years, Brother Rice freshmen were introduced to the football program by one of Al Fracassa's own.

And what did they hear?

"Most of my coaching approach was to try to emulate Coach Fracassa as best I could. To be demanding but always encouraging. To never let a player leave the practice field feeling dejected or hopeless. Al always gave a player the opportunity to redeem himself. I will never forget that about him. He would never ask us to do anything that he did not do himself. Teaching them what was to be expected as they advanced in his program was paramount. My first job was getting those guys to be the best of friends to each other and to trust each other. They are your blood brothers. These will be the friends you will have all your life. They will be the best man at your wedding, the godfathers of your children and the pallbearers at your funeral."

Care to Know More?

If these stories have inspired you, take some time to get to know these organizations that are working to strengthen high school coaching.

Organizations

Positive Coaching Alliance

Founded in 1998 by Jim Thompson at Stanford University, the Positive Coaching Alliance has become the model for a positive approach to coaching. The organization has trained tens of thousands of coaches in the philosophy of relentless positivity. It also sponsors an annual Double-Goal Coach awards competition. Goal No. 1 is preparing athletes to win. Goal No. 2, and the more-important goal, is to teach life lessons through sports.

To learn more about PCA, visit its website at positivecoach.org.

To nominate a coach for the Double-Goal Coach award, you can find applications and deadlines at https://positivecoach.org/awards-programs/double-goal-coach-awards/.

To learn more about Jim Thompson and the organization's founding and history, listen to his interview with me on the Time

Out for Better Coaching Podcast at https://open.spotify.com/episode/6Rn5bWYTEKtHD6GktOvTfU.

I am honored to serve on PCA's Mid-Atlantic Leadership Council.

Play Like A Champion Today

Dedicated to changing the culture of youth sports, Play Like a Champion Today works with a vast network of partners to train coaches and parents. Its program focuses on the core elements of effective coaching: 1) motivation, 2) team-building, and 3) leadership. Founded at the University of Notre Dame, Play Like a Champion is now an independent nonprofit organization.

To learn more about Play Like a Champion Today, visit the website at playlikeachampion.org.

To learn more about the organization and its work, listen to Play Like a Champion's Kristin Sheehan discuss the group's work with me on the Time Out for Better Coaching Podcast at https://open.spotify.com/episode/2uXdIOCJXEuEmXAdeCpmtk.

InCourage

InCourage creates innovative videos that leverage academic research to help athletes, coaches, and parents better understand one another to create a healthy culture. All of InCourage's resources are freely available.

To learn more about InCourage, visit its website at incourage.com.

For an insider's view of the organization, tune in to my conversation with InCourage co-founder Steve Young at the Time Out for Better Coaching Podcast at https://open.spotify.com/episode/4vRSezGF171uYHKaTq3CMu.

The Center for Healing & Justice Through Sport

Sport has a unique ability to captivate children, schools, communities and nations, yet is widely underutilized as a tool for social development. The Center for Healing & Justice Through Sport is proud to contribute to the movement to reimagine the role of sport in our society. Originally founded as We Coach, you can learn more about the organization and its founder, Megan Bartlett, as she talks about her work with me on the Time Out for Better Coaching podcast at https://open.spotify.com/episode/0Q7EvfaQd1DCZ310c81Knr.

Discussion Guide

Books inspire when they are read; they come alive when people talk about them.

This book is meant to be discussed. How you do that depends, in large measure, on the group involved in the discussion. Below are several suggested outlines that can be followed.

For High School Coaching Staffs

The pressure on coaches is ceaseless, and the thought of requiring all coaches to read and discuss this book is probably more than most staffs are able to bear. As constructed, however, staffs can slice and dice these short chapters in order to fit the particular challenges they may be concerned about.

Consider assigning just one section and then meeting for an hour or two, to discuss how the examples provided in this book can benefit your staff. Below are sample questions.

Reading to address a problem

- Of the coaches we read about, which one talks about the problem we're facing in a way we haven't previously considered?

- Can we apply to our current situation the approaches these coaches describe?

- What factors outside of the team motivated the coaches in our reading? What outside factors should we be open to and thinking about?

- What elements in their communities did these coaches pull on in order to get better?

Reading to help bring staff together

- How did Barry Wortman use humility to bring his coaches closer together?

- Looking at Allie Kinniard and Pam Bosser, what can we—as coaches—do to better support one another?

- In reading about Adam Priefer's "learning lab," is there a way to apply that approach to how we develop our coaches?

- The relationship between the coach and athletic director can make or break a team. Pam Bosser has a deep abiding faith in Allie Kinniard. What did Allie do to earn that trust?

Reading for personal development

- Michael Groves has done extensive work in personal development. What organizations could we reach out to that would help us in the same way organizations helped him?

- Tom Generous grew by learning to listen to his players. What are my players telling me that I'm not hearing, and how might I become a better listener?

- Marvin Nash talks about getting to know kids by name and by need. Right now, how many names do I know? How well do I know their needs?

- Gail Maundrell adjusted her approach to gymnastics as club teams took away the best athletes. What is my greatest weakness, and how can I turn it into an advantage?

- Andrew Hyslop stresses that no one owns the athlete. What does this mean, and am I living up to that?

- The line between coach and supportive friend can be a fine one. Nathan Yates seems to instinctively know when to jump from one to the other. How do I draw that line, and how do I judge when to switch from one role to the next?

For Parents of High School Athletes

Parents are going through some difficult changes when their children transition from youth sports to high school sports. While many parents are highly involved in sports when their kids are young, it is often at the high school level that they are required to step back and let the coach—well, coach. It's a change that some parents deal with better than others.

A way to help parents do this is to help them better understand what coaches experience. Having parents read Part II, on coaches and their programs, can help them better understand what their kids are entering. Here are some questions to discuss:

- The chapter on Adam Priefer describes how he is turning his athletes into leaders. As a parent, how important is it for me to step back and let this process happen? When do I know that things are not working well?

- Fernando Gonzalez faced a new situation when he started coaching: women on the men's team. It took him some time to figure out how to deal with that. As a parent, how patient should I be?

- Maurice Henriques talks about pouring into kids. Am I ready to have another adult provide that kind of support for my child?

Learn More

Want to place a group order of books? Contact our publishing house at info@FrontEdgePublishing.com. If you are planning a larger "group read" of 100 or more individuals, ask our publishing house about personalizing that shipment of books for your organization. We could add your logo to the cover, for example. Care to ask a question? Visit our online resource page at ThirtyDaysWith.com. Got news to share? We would enjoy hearing about your community's experience with this book. Please, send us a summary of your experience and include photos if you have them. We often publish newsy updates from across the country in our Front Edge Publishing weekly columns and in our related ReadTheSpirit.com online magazine.

Acknowledgments

A book like this one depends upon the kindness and generosity of hundreds of people. This book would not be possible were it not for the efforts of many individuals.

There is no better place to begin my acknowledgments than with my mother and father, Pat and Martin Davis. They have supported me throughout this project. More importantly, they taught me the beauty and importance of sports, as well as the limits and proper role of sports in one's life. The day that I became a coach, my first call was to them. That says it all.

My fellow coaches at Riverbend High School are family, too. In ways they will never be able to fully appreciate, each has had a profound impact on this work. "Thank you" is too small an expression of gratitude, but I hope that each of the following people knows the depths of appreciation that lie behind those two words: Nathan Yates (head coach), Angelo Sciandra (special teams coordinator), Byron Allen (defensive coordinator), Nat Jackson (offensive coordinator), Rodney Anderson (assistant coach), David Hockney (assistant coach), Stephen Moran (assistant coach), Lance Christmas (assistant coach), Dave Duggan (assistant coach) and Michael Buchert (assistant coach).

Special thanks also must go to Coach Tony DeMarco and Coach McDonald. These two men coached my son Austin at Riverbend High

School. They not only helped him grow into a fine athlete, but they were critical in setting him on a successful life path. Thank you, Tony. And to Coach McDonald, "Semper Fi."

I could write a book about the contributions Howard Brown has made to this project. Howard introduced me to Coach Phil Moresi, but just as important, his energy, encouragement and belief in this project kept me going even when even I doubted it. He saw in me things that I didn't see in myself. The highest honor I can give him is this: "Thanks, Coach."

David Crumm, my editor at Front Edge Publishing and a longtime professional colleague and friend, means more to me and to this project than I can say here. David is a man of few words, so I'll just say, "David—you're simply the best." David's colleague Susan Stitt has done the impossible: She got me on Twitter.

This book would not have happened without the assistance of those who work in state high school athletic associations. These individuals pointed me to many of the people interviewed in this book. Special thanks go to Diane McKay (Texas High School Athletic Directors Association), Matthew Gillespie (Tennessee Secondary School Athletic Association), Tim Stried (Ohio High School Athletic Association) and Kayla Dempsey (North Carolina High School Athletic Association).

Anne Moorman of Atlanta, Georgia, introduced me to Juanda Hislop, who in turn opened a channel for me to interview Clarence Lewis and Andrew Hyslop.

Joe Grimm of Michigan State University put me onto coaches Al Fracassa and Fouad Zaban.

G. Jeffrey McDonald is a longstanding friend in Massachusetts, a former high school athlete and an outstanding journalist. He introduced me to Tom Generous.

Megan Bartlett of The Center for Healing & Justice Through Sport introduced me to Ben Gucciardi and listened to early ideas about how I was planning to frame this book. Her perspective proved informative and is reflected in several places.

Amy Manson, Jake Wald and Jason Sacks, of the Positive Coaching Alliance, introduced me to Maurice Henriques. Each also has offered insights and advice that shaped the final product.

Roy Kessel, Zach Davis, Kristin Sheehan and Shone Evans have honored me with an invitation to their podcasts, giving me space to talk about my passion for coaching and for this book. Each has also become a friend. These individuals have assisted this work in other important ways, too: Opening doors, listening to ideas and advancing the cause.

Nicole Ialeggio (we call her coach I) has been an enormous help. From websites to interviews, social media to sounding board, there aren't enough ways to say "thank you."

Special thanks must go to the many people who helped sustain this project. I am forever thankful for the contributions made by the following: my parents (again), Howard Brown (again), Tracy Norcross, Pam Vessels, Bill Dockery, Carter Macleod, David Pratt, Lora Magruder, Theresa Shouse, Anne Moorman, John Ridley, Ron Reed, Vinay Sekhar, Wilma Dague, Jeff MacDonald, Molly Wade, Veronica McConnell, Baghesri Gate and David Briggs.

Finally, I wish to thank the 30 people who are the voices and faces that make up this book. They opened up their playbooks—and oftentimes their hearts—when sharing the details of their coaching journeys. We are a better nation, and better people, because of them—and the thousands more whose names won't be immortalized in print.

Recommended Reading

Thirty Days with Abraham Lincoln

by Duncan Newcomer

Abraham Lincoln is the soul of America, calling us to our best as Americans. Duncan Newcomer has hosted more than 200 episodes of the radio series Quiet Fire: The Spiritual Life of Abraham Lincoln. Now, 30 of his best stories provide a month of inspirational reading in a unique volume that also lets readers listen to original broadcasts each day.

Thirty Days with King David

by Larry Buxton

In turbulent times, King David united a nation—and his hard-earned wisdom can bring us together today. David ranks among the world's greatest heroes for defeating Goliath and best-selling authors for writing Psalms. He is honored by Jews, Christians and Muslims. In this book, pastor, educator and leadership coach Larry Buxton shows us how David embodies 14 crucial values shared by effective leaders to this day.

Find these books on Amazon.com, BarnesandNoble.com, Walmart.com, AbeBooks.com and other retailers. eBook formats available.

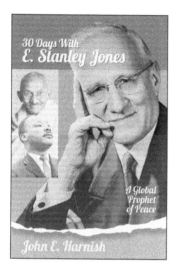

Thirty Days with E. Stanley Jones

by John Harnish

In 1964, when E. Stanley Jones was 80 years old, *TIME* magazine compared his international reputation as a Christian leader to Billy Graham. Throughout the early and mid-20th century, E. Stanley Jones was one of the best-known Christian voices in the world. A counselor to presidents and a close friend of Mahatma Gandhi, his influence reached far beyond the U.S. and his adopted homeland of India.

To My Professor:
Student Voices for Great College Teaching

by the Michigan State University
School of Journalism

Find out what students have to say about college teaching. These are not the remarks you usually see on feedback forms, and some are harsh. Others are full of gratitude for professors who inspire and motivate. These statements lead to advice from master teachers who are helping drive innovation in university-level pedagogy.

CPSIA information can be obtained
at www.ICGtesting.com
Printed in the USA
LVHW041242090222
710560LV00005B/422